MW01488905

A source book of company secretarial documents and precedents

Contents

Introduction

This book contains, in one volume, precedents for the documentation required for most transactions likely to arise during the lifetime of a private company. It is also designed as a practical guide to the preparation of board and general meeting minutes and resolutions. Each precedent is numbered and wherever possible the notes relating to the precedent will be found on the opposite left hand page. The precedents have been prepared in A4 format to facilitate photocopying for use in the office.

This book is not intended to be a substitute for a legal textbook, and reference should, therefore, be made to such for details of the law governing any transaction to be documented.

Capital duty was abolished in the 1988 Budget, but at the date of publication there have been no changes to Forms PUC1, PUC2, PUC3, PUC4, PUC5 and PUC7 and these forms are at the time of writing still required to be filed at the Registry. However, it is likely that the PUC forms will be changed in the near future and certain of them may be discontinued.

Abbreviations and definitions

the Act	The Companies Act 1985
the Registrar	The Registrar of Companies for England and Wales or for Scotland as the case may be (dependent upon the country of the situation of the registered office of the company).
Table A (or B, C, D, E or F)	Table A (or B, C, D, E or F) contained in The Companies (Tables A to F) Regulations 1985 (SI 1985/805) (as amended by SI 1985/1052).
CDDA	Company Directors Disqualification Act 1985
CP	Companies Consolidation (Consequential Provisions) Act 1985
ID	Companies Securities (Insider Dealing) Act 1985
s.	section

Notes: References in this book to any section numbers without specific reference to an Act shall be references to the Companies Act 1985.

References in this book to Table A are to the Table A defined above. This form of Table A applies to companies incorporated on or after 1 August 1985 and to other companies expressly adopting this form of Table A (see **1.1**). The form of Table A set out in SI 1985/805 (without the amendments made by SI 1985/1052) is applicable to companies incorporated between 1 July and 31 July 1985, unless another form is expressly adopted.

The applicable form of Table A for companies incorporated prior to 1 July 1985 will be the version contained in the Companies Act in force at the date of the company's incorporation. The pre-1985 forms of Table A differ both as regards content and numbering of regulations – the text and precedents in this book should accordingly be read as subject to any variations necessitated by application of a pre-1985 form of Table A.

1 Matters arising on and following incorporation

CONTENTS

NOTES ON 1.1

The memorandum of association must be in the relevant statutory form (Table B for private companies or Table F for public companies) or as near thereto as circumstances admit. The following clauses must be contained in a company's memorandum:

1. The name of the company.
2. That the company is to be a public company (if that is the case).
3. Whether the registered office is to be situated in England and Wales or in Scotland.
4. The objects of the company.
5. That the liability is limited.
6. The amount of the share capital and its division into shares of a fixed amount.

The memorandum ends with a formal subscription clause which is set out in the statutory forms.

The memorandum of association in **1.1** is suitable for a private company limited by shares.

The name of the company must be inserted in the heading and in clause 1.

The main objects (main business to be conducted by the company) must be set out in clause 3 (a).

The amount of the authorised share capital, the number of shares and the amount of each share should be set out in clause 5. Even if there are different classes of shares it is usual not to refer to these in this clause. Normally a clause would be added to the articles of association setting out the authorised share capital of the company and its division into the various classes of shares. The rights attaching to such shares would then also be set out in the articles of association.

The memorandum must be signed by at least two persons who thereby agree to take up the number of shares set against their names. Each must take a minimum of one share.

MEMORANDUM OF ASSOCIATION

THE COMPANIES ACT 1985

A PRIVATE COMPANY LIMITED BY SHARES

MEMORANDUM OF ASSOCIATION

OF

1. The Company's name is

2. The Company's registered office is to be situated in England and Wales.

3. The Company's objects are:

(a)

(b) to carry on any other trade or business whatever, which can in the opinion of the directors be advantageously carried on in connection with or ancillary to any of the businesses of the Company;

(c) to purchase, take on lease or in exchange, hire or otherwise acquire and hold for any estate or interest any lands, buildings, easements, rights, privileges, concessions, patents, patent rights, licences, secret processes, machinery, plant, stock-in-trade, and any real or personal property of any kind necessary or convenient for the purposes of or in connection with the Company's business or any branch or department thereof;

(d) to erect, construct, lay down, enlarge, alter and maintain any roads, railways, tramways, sidings, bridges, reservoirs, shops, stores, factories, buildings, works, plant and machinery necessary or convenient for the Company's business, and to contribute to or subsidise the erection, construction and maintenance of any of the above;

(e) to borrow or raise or secure the payment of money for the purposes of or in connection with the Company's business, and for the purposes of or in connection with the borrowing or raising of money by the Company to become a member of any building society;

(f) to mortgage and charge the undertaking and all or any of the real and personal property and assets, present or future, and all or any of the uncalled capital for the time being of the Company, and to issue at par or at a premium or discount, and for such consideration and with and subject to such rights, powers, privileges and conditions as may be thought fit, debentures or

FOR NOTES TO 1.1 SEE PAGE 2

debenture stock, either permanent or redeemable or repayable, and collaterally or further to secure any securities of the Company by a trust deed or other assurances;

(g) to issue and deposit any securities which the Company has power to issue by way of mortgage, and also by way of security for the performance of any contracts or obligations of the Company or of its customers or other persons or corporations having dealings with the Company, or in whose businesses or undertakings the Company is interested, whether directly or indirectly;

(h) to receive money on deposit or loan upon such terms as the Company may approve, and to guarantee the obligations and contracts of customers and others;

(i) to lend money to any company, firm or person and to give all kinds of indemnities and either with or without the Company receiving any consideration or advantage, direct or indirect, for giving any such guarantee, to guarantee either by personal covenant or by mortgaging or charging all or any part of the undertaking, property and assets present and future and uncalled capital of the Company or by both such methods, the performance of the obligations and the payment of the capital or principal (together with any premium) of and dividends or interest on any debenture stocks, shares or other securities of any company, firm or person and in particular (but without limiting the generality of the foregoing) any company which is for the time being the Company's holding or subsidiary company as defined by section 736 of the Companies Act 1985 or otherwise associated with the Company in business and whether or not this Company receives directly or indirectly any consideration or advantage therefrom;

(j) to establish and maintain or procure the establishment and maintenance of any non-contributory or contributory pension or superannuation funds for the benefit of, and give or procure the giving of donations, gratuities, pensions, allowances, or emoluments to any persons who are or were at any time in the employment or service of the Company, or of any company which is for the time being the Company's holding or subsidiary company as defined by section 736 of the Companies Act 1985 or otherwise associated with the Company in business or who are or were at the time directors or officers of the Company or of any such other company as aforesaid, and the wives, widows, families and dependants of any such persons, and also to establish and subsidise or subscribe to any institutions, associations, clubs or funds calculated to be for the benefit of or to advance the interests and well-being of the Company or of any such other company as aforesaid, or of any such persons as aforesaid, and to make payments for or towards the insurance of any such persons as aforesaid, and to subscribe or guarantee money for charitable or benevolent objects or for any exhibition or for any public, general or useful object; and to establish, set up, support and maintain share purchase schemes or profit-sharing schemes for the benefit of any employees of the Company or of any company which is for the time being the Company's holding or subsidiary company as defined by section 736 of the Companies Act 1985 and to do any of the matters aforesaid, either alone on in conjunction with any such other company as aforesaid;

(k) to draw, make, accept, endorse, negotiate, discount and execute promissory notes, bills of exchange and other negotiable instruments;

(l) to invest and deal with the moneys of the Company not immediately required for the purposes of its business in or upon such investments or securities and in any such manner as may from time to time be determined;

FOR NOTES TO 1.1 SEE PAGE 2

(m) to pay for any property or rights acquired by the Company, either in cash or in fully or partly paid-up shares, with or without preferred or deferred or special rights or restrictions in respect of dividend, repayment of capital, voting or otherwise, or by any securities which the Company has power to issue, or partly in one mode and partly in another, and generally on such terms as the Company may determine;

(n) to accept payment for any property or rights sold or otherwise disposed of or dealt with by the Company, either in cash, by instalments or otherwise, or in fully or partly paid-up shares of any company or corporation, with or without deferred or preferred or special rights or restrictions in respect of dividend, repayment of capital, voting or otherwise, or in debentures or mortgage debentures or debenture stock, mortgages or other securities of any company or corporation, or partly in one mode and partly in another, and generally on such terms as the Company may determine, and to hold, dispose of or otherwise deal with any shares, stock or securities so acquired;

(o) to enter into any partnership or joint-purse arrangement or arrangement for sharing profits, union of interests or co-operation with any company, firm or person carrying on or proposing to carry on any business within the objects of this Company, and to acquire and hold, sell, deal with or dispose of shares, stocks or securities of any such company, and to guarantee the contracts or liabilities of, or the payment of the dividends, interest or capital of any shares, stock or securities of and to subsidise or otherwise assist any such company;

(p) to establish or promote or concur in establishing or promoting any other company whose objects shall include the acquisition and taking over of all or any of the assets and liabilities of the Company or the promotion of which shall be in any manner calculated to advance directly or indirectly the objects or interests of this Company, and to acquire and hold or dispose of shares, stock or securities and guarantee the payment of dividends, interest or capital of any shares, stock or securities issued by or any other obligations of any such company;

(q) to purchase or otherwise acquire and undertake all or any part of the business, property, assets, liabilities and transactions of any person, firm or company carrying on any business which this Company is authorised to carry on;

(r) to sell, improve, manage, develop, turn to account, exchange, let on rent, royalty, share of profits or otherwise, grant licences, easements and other rights in or over, and in any other manner deal with or dispose of the undertaking and all or any of the property and assets for the time being of the Company for such consideration as the Company may think fit;

(s) to amalgamate with any other company whose objects are or include objects similar to those of this Company, whether by sale or purchase (for fully or partly paid-up shares or otherwise) of the undertaking, subject to the liabilities of this or any such other company as aforesaid, with or without winding up, or by sale or purchase (for fully or partly paid-up shares or otherwise) of all or a controlling interest in the shares or stock of this or any such other company as aforesaid, or by partnership, or any arrangement of the nature of partnership, or in any other manner;

(t) to subscribe or guarantee money for or organise or assist any national, local, charitable, benevolent, public, general or useful object, or for any exhibition or for any purpose which may be considered likely directly or indirectly to further the objects of the Company or the interests of its members;

FOR NOTES TO 1.1 SEE PAGE 2

(u) to distribute among the members in specie any property of the Company, or any proceeds of sale or disposal of any property of the Company, but so that no distribution amounting to a reduction of capital be made except with the sanction (if any) for the time being required by law;

(v) to give such financial assistance, directly or indirectly, for the purpose of the acquisition of shares in the Company or the Company's holding company as defined by section 736 of the Companies Act 1985 or for the purpose of reducing or discharging any liability incurred by any person for the purpose of the acquisition of shares in the Company or the Company's holding company as defined by section 736 of the Companies Act 1985 as may be lawful;

(w) to do all or any of the above things in any part of the world, and either as principals, agents, trustees, contractors or otherwise, and either alone or in conjunction with others, and either by or through agents, trustees, sub-contractors or otherwise;

(x) to do all such things as are incidental or conducive to the above objects or any of them.

And it is hereby declared that the objects of the Company as specified in each of the foregoing paragraphs of this clause (except only if and so far as otherwise expressly provided in any paragraphs) shall be separate and distinct objects of the Company and shall not be in any way limited by reference to any other paragraph or the name of the Company.

4. The liability of the members is limited.

5. The Company's share capital is £   divided into   shares of £   each.

FOR NOTES TO 1.1 SEE PAGE 2

We, the subscribers to this memorandum of association, wish to be formed into a Company pursuant to this memorandum; and we agree to take the number of shares shown opposite our respective names.

NAMES AND ADDRESSES OF SUBSCRIBERS	Number of shares taken by each subscriber
Total shares taken	

Dated the   day of   , 19   .

Witness to the above signatures:

NOTES ON 1.2

The articles of association govern a company's internal affairs. They must be divided into consecutively numbered paragraphs and, in the case of articles registered at the time of incorporation, be signed by the subscribers. A model set of articles is contained in Table A. The articles in **1.2** adopt Table A with certain modifications.

Article 1

This provides that Table A will apply to the company as modified by the articles in **1.2**.

Article 2

This provides that the shares will be under the control of the directors to allot as they think fit and gives the directors authority to allot relevant securities for a period of five years from the date of the incorporation of the company. It should be noted that if the share capital of the company is increased above the level with which it was incorporated this authority must be renewed prior to any allotment of shares by the directors (see **3.2** resolution 2). Paragraph (d) waives the statutory pre-emption rights contained in sections 89 and 90 of the Act.

If it is intended that the directors should allot shares on a pro rata basis, clause 2(a) can be replaced (see **1.3** for a suggested article).

Article 3

This extends the company's lien contained in regulation 8 of Table A.

Article 4

This clause gives the directors an absolute discretion to refuse to register a transfer of shares and widens regulation 24 of Table A. A number of alternative transfer provisions can be found in Chapter 4.

Article 5

This clause alters regulation 41 of Table A and provides that if a quorum is not present at an adjourned meeting the meeting will be dissolved.

Article 6

Regulation 64 of Table A provides that there shall be a minimum number of two directors. This regulation has been deleted by article 1 of these articles. Regulation 6 provides for a minimum of one director. A sole director may not also act as secretary.

Article 7

This facilitates the appointment of directors who need not retire by rotation. If required the retirement by rotation provisions can be deleted altogether and an alternative article could be inserted as follows:

'The directors shall not be required to retire by rotation and regulations 76 to 80 shall be modified accordingly.'

Regulations 73 to 75 of Table A should then be excluded from applying to the company and this should be provided for in article 1 of the articles.

Article 8

This article enables the directors to borrow money without limit. There is no longer any regulation specifically dealing with directors' borrowing powers in

ARTICLES OF ASSOCIATION

THE COMPANIES ACT 1985

A PRIVATE COMPANY LIMITED BY SHARES

ARTICLES OF ASSOCIATION

OF

PRELIMINARY

1. The regulations contained in Table A in the Schedule to the Companies (Tables A to F) Regulations 1985 as amended by the Companies (Tables A to F) (Amendment) Regulations 1985 (such Table being hereinafter referred to as 'Table A') shall apply to the Company save in so far as they are excluded or varied hereby: that is to say, clauses 8 and 64 of Table A shall not apply to the Company; and in addition to the remaining clauses of Table A, as varied hereby, the following shall be the articles of association of the Company.

SHARES

2. (a) Subject to sub-article (b) hereof all shares shall be under the control of the directors and the directors may allot, grant options over, or otherwise deal with or dispose of the same to such persons and generally on such terms and in such manner as they think fit.

    (b) The directors are generally and unconditionally authorised for the purposes of section 80 of the Act to allot relevant securities (as defined in section 80 of the Act) provided that the aggregate nominal value of such securities allotted pursuant to this authority shall not exceed the amount of the authorised share capital with which the Company is incorporated; and that this authority shall expire on the fifth anniversary of the incorporation of the Company unless varied or revoked or renewed by the Company in general meeting.

    (c) The directors shall be entitled under the authority conferred by this article to make at any time before the expiry of such authority any offer or agreement which will or may require relevant securities to be allotted after the expiry of such authority.

    (d) In accordance with section 91 of the Act, section 89(1) and section 90(1) to (6) of the Act shall not apply to any allotment of equity securities (as defined in section 94 of the Act) by the Company.

3. The Company shall have a first and paramount lien on every share (whether or not it is a fully paid share) for all moneys (whether presently payable or not) called or payable at a fixed time in respect of that share and the Company shall also have a first and paramount lien on all shares (whether fully paid or not) standing registered in the name of any person whether solely or as one of two or more joint holders for all moneys presently payable by him or his estate to the Company; but the directors may at any time declare any share to be wholly or in part exempt from the provisions of this article. The Company's lien on a share shall extend to any dividend or other amount payable in respect thereof.

NOTES ON 1.2 (CONTD)

Table A since it is considered to be within their general powers conferred by regulation 70 of Table A. However, most banks still insist upon such an article prior to providing a company with any borrowing facilities.

Article 9

This article enables directors to vote upon resolutions concerning contracts in which they have an interest. However, the directors must still comply with section 317 of the Act.

Article 10

This article widens the indemnity provisions of regulation 118 of Table A.

TRANSFER OF SHARES

4. The directors may, in their absolute discretion, and without assigning any reason therefor, decline to register any transfer of any share, whether or not it is a fully paid share; and regulation 24 of Table A shall be modified accordingly.

5. Regulation 41 of Table A shall be read and construed as if the last sentence ended with the words: 'and if at the adjourned meeting a quorum is not present within half an hour from the time appointed for the meeting, the meeting shall be dissolved'.

DIRECTORS

6. Unless and until the Company in general meeting shall otherwise determine, there shall not be any limitation as to the number of directors. If and so long as there is a sole director, he may exercise all the powers and authorities vested in the directors by these articles or Table A; and regulation 89 of Table A shall be modified accordingly.

7. If the resolution or instrument by which a director is appointed so provides, he shall be a permanent director and not subject to retirement by rotation; and regulations 73 to 75 (inclusive) of Table A shall not apply to any permanent director.

8. The directors may exercise all the powers of the Company to borrow money, and to mortgage or charge its undertaking, property, and uncalled capital, or any part thereof, and to issue debentures, debenture stock, and other securities whether outright or as a security for any debt, liability or obligation of the Company or of any third party.

9. A director may vote as a director on any resolution concerning any contract or arrangement in which he is interested or upon any matter arising thereout, and if he shall so vote his vote shall be counted and he shall be reckoned in estimating a quorum when any such contract or arrangement is under consideration; and regulation 94 of Table A shall be modified accordingly.

INDEMNITY

10. Subject to the provisions of the Act and in addition to such indemnity as is contained in regulation 118 of Table A, every director, officer or official of the Company shall be entitled to be indemnified out of the assets of the Company against all losses or liabilities incurred by him in or about the execution and discharge of the duties of his office.

FOR NOTES TO 1.2 SEE PAGE 12

NAMES AND ADDRESSES OF SUBSCRIBERS

Dated the   day of   , 19   .

Witness to the above signatures:

NOTES ON 1.3, 1.4, 1.5, 1.6 AND 1.7

The precedents referred to above can be inserted as additional or alternative articles to the articles of association in **1.2**.

1.3 can be inserted as an alternative clause to article 2(a). Article 2(a) provides that the shares will be under the control of the directors to allot as they think fit; **1.3** restricts the directors' ability to allot shares by providing that such shares must be offered to the existing members on a pro rata basis unless the company by ordinary resolution otherwise directs.

If this clause is inserted into a company's articles the words 'and unconditionally' should be deleted from article 2(b) in **1.2**

1.4 can be inserted as a new article 6 and the remaining articles should be re-numbered accordingly and regulation 54 of Table A should be excluded from applying to the company.

This article sets out the voting rights attaching to the shares in the company and further gives the directors enhanced voting rights if a resolution is proposed to remove a director from office (see *Bushell* v. *Faith* [1970] A.C. 1099). The effect of this article is that the directors of the company will be permanent and cannot be removed by the company in general meeting.

Paragraphs (2) and (3) must be completed to show the number of votes to which a director should be entitled. The figure inserted should be sufficient to enable him to outvote the remaining members of the company.

1.5 could be inserted as a new article 8 and the remaining articles in **1.2** should be re-numbered accordingly. This article enables the company to remove a director from office by extraordinary resolution. The inclusion of such an article avoids the necessity of special notice (28 days) which is provided for in s.303. However, the provisions of s.303 would still apply to the company and therefore the company could still remove a director pursuant to that section.

1.6 could be inserted also as a new article 8 or alternatively if **1.5** is also included in the company's articles as article 9, and the remaining articles should be re-numbered accordingly. This provision can be useful if the company is a subsidiary of another company since it provides that the holding company can appoint and remove directors simply by written notice.

1.7 could be inserted as a new article 6, and the remaining articles should be re-numbered accordingly. Regulation 50 of Table A should also be excluded from applying to the company and article 1 should therefore also be altered. This provision provides that the chairman at both general and directors' meetings will not be entitled to a second or casting vote.

PRE-EMPTION ON ALLOTMENT OF SHARES

1. Any shares proposed to be issued shall first be offered to the members holding shares of the same class in proportion as nearly as may be to the number of shares of that class held by them respectively, unless the company shall by ordinary resolution otherwise direct.

2. The offer shall be made by notice specifying the number of shares offered, and limiting a period (not being less than twenty-one days) within which the offer, if not accepted, will be deemed to be declined.

3. After the expiration of that period, those shares declined or so deemed to be declined shall be offered in the proportions aforesaid to the persons who have, within the said period, accepted all the shares offered to them, such further offer shall be made in the same manner and limited by a like period as the original offer.

4. Any shares not accepted pursuant to such offer or further offer as aforesaid and any shares released from the provisions of this article by such ordinary resolution as aforesaid or which by reason of the proportion borne by them to the number of persons entitled to such offer as aforesaid or by reason of any other difficulty in apportioning the same, cannot in the opinion of the directors be conveniently offered in the manner hereinbefore provided shall be under the control of the directors, who may allot, grant options over or otherwise dispose of the same to such persons, on such terms, and in such manner as they think fit, provided that, in the case of shares not accepted as aforesaid, such shares shall not be disposed of on terms which are more favourable to the subscribers thereof than the terms on which they were offered to the members.

FOR NOTES TO 1.3, 1.4, 1.5, 1.6 AND 1.7 SEE PAGE 18

ENHANCED VOTING RIGHTS

1. Subject to paragraphs (2) and (3) below, on a show of hands every member who (being an individual) is present in person or (being a corporation) is present by a duly authorised representative, not being himself a member entitled to vote, shall have one vote and on a poll every member shall have one vote for every share of which he is the holder.

2. If at any general meeting a poll is duly demanded on a resolution to remove a director from office, the director named in the resolution shall be entitled to   votes for each share of which he is the holder.

3. If at any general meeting a poll is duly demanded on a resolution to delete or amend the provisions of this article, every director shall have   votes for each share of which he is the holder if voting against such a resolution.

FOR NOTES TO 1.3, 1.4, 1.5, 1.6 AND 1.7 SEE PAGE 18

REMOVAL OF DIRECTORS

Without prejudice to the provisions of section 303, Companies Act 1985, the company may, by extraordinary resolution, remove a director before the expiration of his period of office notwithstanding anything in these articles or in any agreement between the company and such director.

FOR NOTES TO 1.3, 1.4, 1.5, 1.6 AND 1.7 SEE PAGE 18

APPOINTMENT OF DIRECTORS – HOLDING COMPANY

If so long as the majority of the issued share capital for the time being of the company is beneficially owned by another body corporate, the directors of the company or any of them may be appointed and removed by written notice served on the company by the beneficial owner for the time being of such amount of the equity capital of the company.

FOR NOTES TO 1.3, 1.4, 1.5, 1.6 AND 1.7 SEE PAGE 18

REMOVAL OF CHAIRMAN'S CASTING VOTE

The chairman shall not, in the event of an equality of votes at any general meeting of the company, or at any meeting of the directors or of a committee of directors, have a second or casting vote. Regulation 88 of Table A shall be modified accordingly.

NOTES ON 1.8

1.8 contains a checklist of matters to be dealt with following incorporation.

On incorporation the subscribers should be entered in the register of members as the holders of the shares subscribed (s.22(1)); no formal allotment is needed of these shares and they should not be included on a return of allotments. However, if these shares were issued nil or partly paid, form PUC5 must be filed with the Registrar within one month of the payment of the shares.

CHECKLIST OF MATTERS ARISING FOLLOWING INCORPORATION OF COMPANY

1. The first directors, secretary and registered office will be stated in the form 10 filed on incorporation.

2. Obtain seal and arrange for the directors (at the first board meeting) to adopt as the common seal and to lay down any necessary regulations for the use of the seal and attestation of sealed documents.

3. The directors should:

    (a) appoint a chairman of the board and, if relevant, managing director;
    (b) appoint the company's bankers and adopt the resolutions set out in the opening of account mandate;
    (c) appoint auditors;
    (d) determine the company's accounting reference date;
    (e) make any necessary allotments of share capital;
    (f) approve the sealing and issue of share certificates arising from (e) above;
    (g) dispense with the distinguishing numbers of all issued fully paid shares in the company, if appropriate (s.182(2));
    (h) appoint persons to represent the company at meetings of members or creditors of other companies (s.375).

4. File return of allotments with the Registrar within one month of any allotments of shares (3(e) above) (form PUC2 for allotments for cash or form PUC3 for allotments for consideration other than cash).

5. Within six months of date of incorporation, give notice of accounting reference date to the Registrar on form 224 (unless the date is 31 March) (3(d) above).

6. Obtain Companies Act registers for the company (e.g. a combined register, preferably in looseleaf form, available from law stationers) and make all necessary entries.

7. Notify place where statutory books are situated if not at registered office (forms 325 or 353).

8. Notify place where directors' service contracts are kept if not at registered office (form 318).

9. Obtain necessary headed stationery for the company and arrange for the full name of the company to be shown outside every place of its business.

10. Consider the need for service agreements for directors/senior executives (e.g. including provisions regarding non-competition with the company).

11. Consider arrangements regarding corporation tax, income tax (PAYE), National Insurance and value added tax, if relevant.

12. Consider the need for the company's property to be insured.

NOTES ON 1.9

If a company is required immediately, one can be purchased from registration agents or from firms of solicitors or accountants which maintain a stock of ready-made ('off the shelf') companies.

In order to incorporate the company in the first instance, the agent will use its nominees to act as first subscribers to the memorandum and as first director and secretary. Prior to the release of the certificate of incorporation the agent will normally require the purchaser to complete and sign forms 287 and 288 to change the registered office of the company and to record the resignation of the agents' nominees as director and secretary and appoint the new directors and secretary.

Some advisers or agents adopt the practice of obtaining waivers from nominee subscribers, the whole of the company's capital being then allotted to other persons; this practice is not to be recommended and transfers should be obtained in respect of the relevant shares. The subscribers should be entered in the register of members as the original holders of the shares.

If such a company has been purchased the matters listed in **1.9** may need to be dealt with, in addition to the matters listed in **1.8**.

CHECKLIST OF MATTERS ARISING FOLLOWING THE ACQUISITION OF A READY-MADE (OFF THE SHELF) COMPANY

1.   Note receipt of letters of resignation of initial directors and secretary and confirm appointment of new directors and secretary and change in registered office.

2.   Approve share transfers transferring the subscribers' shares and arrange for payment of these shares if issued nil paid on incorporation. (Usually registration agent will provide that shares are transferred in consideration of the transferee paying the nominal value for such shares to the company.)

3.   Consider change of company name and any alterations to the memorandum and articles of association. If any of these changes are to be made an extraordinary general meeting of the company must be held (see **1.12**, **1.14**, **1.15** and **1.16**).

NOTES ON 1.10

1.10 is an example of a notice of board meeting and agenda. However, there is no requirement to give written notice of board meetings and further, there is no minimum period of notice, although it must be reasonable in the circumstances.

Section 382 provides that a company must keep minutes of all proceedings of meetings of its directors (see **1.11**). Any minute signed by the chairman of a meeting or the chairman of the next succeeding meeting is evidence of the proceedings.

NOTICE OF BOARD MEETING AND AGENDA

To the directors of   Limited

NOTICE OF BOARD MEETING

The first meeting of the directors of   Limited will be held at
             on   commencing at   for the
transaction of the following business:

1.   To report the incorporation of the company.

2.   To appoint the chairman.

3.   To appoint (additional) directors.

4.   To adopt a common seal.

5.   To open an account at   Bank plc.

6.   To appoint auditors.

7.   To determine the company's accounting reference date.

8.   To allot further shares.

9.   To produce notices given by   and   pursuant
      to section 317 of the Companies Act 1985.

Yours sincerely,

Secretary

NOTES ON 1.11

If a ready-made company has been acquired the board minutes in **1.11** can be utilised with certain amendments.

Minutes 1 and 2 should be replaced with the following:

'1. There were produced the certificate of incorporation of the company (No.   ) dated   19   , a print of the memorandum and articles of association as registered, two stock transfer forms of the subscribers' shares, the notice of appointment of the new directors and resignation of the first director(s), the notice of resignation of the first secretary and appointment of new secretary and resolution of change of registered office.'

Minute 6 should be amended to delete the reference to the secretary being appointed in the statement delivered to the Registrar and minute 7 should be deleted.

It may be necessary to include the following additional resolution if changes are to be made to the company's name, share capital or memorandum or articles of association:

'There was produced to the meeting a notice of extraordinary general meeting together with a form of consent to short notice duly signed by the requisite number of members for the purposes of:

(a) increasing the authorised share capital and conferring authority on the directors to allot shares pursuant to s.80;

(b) changing the name of the company to   Limited;

(c) altering the memorandum of association to enable the company to carry on the business of   ;

(d) adopting new articles of asociation.

It was resolved that the notice be approved and the secretary be instructed to serve the notice on the members and that they be asked to agree to the holding of the meeting on short notice.'

The following should replace minute 12:

'It was resolved:
THAT the undermentioned transfers of the subscribers' shares, having been stamped and duly executed by both the transferor and the transferee, be approved and registered and that the sum of £1 on each having been duly called be paid up immediately and that share certificates in respect of such shares be sealed and issued:

Name of transferee   Name of transferor   No. of shares   .'

MINUTES OF FIRST BOARD MEETING

LIMITED

Minutes of a meeting of the board of directors held at
on   19   , at   a.m./p.m.

Present: (Chairman)

In attendance:

1.   There were produced the certificate of incorporation of the company
     (No.   ) dated   19   , and a print of the memorandum
     and articles of association as registered.

2.   It was noted that   and   had been named by the subscribers as
     the first directors of the company in the statement delivered to the Registrar
     with the memorandum.

3.   and   took their seats on the board.

4.   It was resolved:
     THAT   be appointed chairman of the board.

5.   took the chair.

6.   The appointment of   as secretary in the statement delivered to the
     Registrar with the memorandum was reported and it was resolved:
     THAT the appointment of   as secretary of the company be
     confirmed [at a salary payable from   19   at the rate of
     £   per annum, such appointment being terminable by three months'
     notice in writing given by either party to the other at any time].

7.   It was resolved:
     THAT the situation of the registered office of the company, namely,
              , shown in the statement delivered with the memorandum
     to the Registrar, be confirmed.

8.   It was resolved:
     THAT the seal, of which an impression is affixed in the margin hereof, be
     adopted as the common seal of the company.

9.   The appointment of bankers was considered and it was resolved:
     THAT the resolutions set out in the bank's printed form (a copy of which is
     attached hereto) be passed.

10. It was resolved:
     THAT   , chartered accountants, be appointed auditors of the
     company to hold office until the conclusion of the first general meeting at
     which accounts are laid before the company.

11. Notices dated   19   , given by   and   pursuant
     to section 317(3) of the Companies Act 1985, were produced and read to the
     meeting.

12. There was produced a form of application dated   19   ,
     from   for   shares of £1 each in the capital of the company at a price
     of £   per share, together with cheques for a total of £   , being payment in
     full for the said   shares and for the 2 shares taken by the subscribers to the
     memorandum of association.

FOR NOTES TO 1.11 SEE PAGE 34

It was resolved:

(a) THAT   shares of £1 each, fully paid and numbered from   to inclusive be allotted to   .

(b) THAT the undermentioned share certificates drawn in respect of the subscribers' shares and the allotment made by resolution (a) hereof be approved and that the common seal be affixed thereto:

No. 1	1 share numbered 1
No. 2	1 share numbered 2
No. 3	shares numbered from to inclusive

13. It was resolved:

THAT so long as all the issued and fully paid ordinary shares of the company rank *pari passu* in all respects distinguishing numbers for the ordinary shares shall not be maintained.

14. The secretary was authorised to purchase books and stationery necessary for the company's business.

15. It was decided to hold the next board meeting at 10 a.m. on   day, 19   .

16. There being no further business the meeting terminated.

NOTES ON 1.12

The name of a company may be changed by special resolution and the procedure is as follows:

1. The proposed new name should be checked against the Registrar's index.

2. A board meeting should be held to convene an extraordinary general meeting (see **7.1.26** for board minute) to consider the special resolution.

3. 21 clear days' notice of the meeting must be given to the members entitled thereto in the form contained in **1.12**.

4. A copy of the special resolution (see **8.10** for form) should be available for signature by the chairman of the meeting and filing with the Registrar within 15 days after it is passed together with a cheque for £40 in respect of the change of name fee.

5. The Registrar will issue a certificate of incorporation on change of name, and the change of name takes effect from the date of the issue of the certificate.

6. A new common seal should be obtained and submitted for adoption by the board of directors (see **7.1.11**).

7. A print of the special resolution should be attached to all copies of the memorandum and articles or alternatively the memorandum and articles should be reprinted, although this is considered not necessary since changing a company's name does not strictly alter its memorandum.

NOTICE CONVENING EXTRAORDINARY GENERAL MEETING TO CHANGE COMPANY NAME

LIMITED

NOTICE IS HEREBY GIVEN that an extraordinary general meeting of the above-named company will be held at   on   19   , at   a.m./p.m. for the purpose of considering and, if thought fit, passing the following resolution as a SPECIAL RESOLUTION:

SPECIAL RESOLUTION

THAT the name of the company be changed to '   LIMITED'

BY ORDER OF THE BOARD

Secretary

Dated

Registered office

Note: A member entitled to attend and vote at the meeting is entitled to appoint a proxy to attend and vote instead of him. A proxy need not be a member of the company.

NOTES ON 1.13

If a company carries on business in Great Britain under a name which does not consist of its corporate name without any addition (other than an indication that the business is carried on in succession to a former owner of the business), the use of the business name is controlled by the provisions of the Business Names Act 1985 as follows:

1. The written approval of the Secretary of State is required for use of a name which implies a connection with central or local government or contains certain words or expressions. (See *Notes for Guidance on Company and Business Names* available from the Registry.)

2. Where the business name is used on business letters, written orders for the supply of goods or services, invoices and receipts or written demands for payment of debts arising in the course of the business, there must also be stated in legible characters the full name of the company and an address within Great Britain at which service of any document relating in any way to the business will be effective (this will generally be the registered office).

3. The information described in (2) above must also be displayed prominently so that it can be read easily in all premises where the business is carried on and to which customers and suppliers have access (see **1.13**) and it must also on request be given immediately in writing to any person with whom anything is done or discussed in the course of the business.

If the above provisions are not complied with, the company and any officers responsible are liable to criminal penalties and the company may suffer civil disabilities in enforcing contracts made in the course of such non-compliance (see the Business Names Act 1985 ss. 4, 5 and 7).

It should be noted that business names are not subject to comparison with names on the index of names of companies kept pursuant to s.714. However care is still needed regarding the use of business names to avoid possible liability for infringement of trademarks or for passing off.

PARTICULARS OF BUSINESS NAME

PURSUANT TO SECTION 4 OF THE BUSINESS NAMES ACT 1985

PARTICULARS OF BUSINESS NAME

Name under which business is carried on

Proprietor(s)

Insert full name(s)

Address within Great Britain at which documents may be effectively served on the business

Insert full address

NOTES ON 1.14 AND RESOLUTION 1 OF 1.16

The objects clause may be altered by special resolution in accordance with s.5 of the Act. The procedure is as follows:

1. A board meeting should be held to convene an extraordinary general meeting to consider the special resolution (see **7.1.26** for board minute).

2. If it is intended to alter the main objects clause (clause 3(a) of the memorandum of association) the resolution proposed should be in the form of **1.14** and this will set out the textual amendment in the notice. If an entirely new clause 3 is to be adopted, the resolution proposed should be in the form of resolution 1 of **1.16**, and the revised clause 3 should be attached to the notice or be available for inspection at the registered office of the company during the period from the date of the notice to the date of the meeting.

3. Notice of the meeting must be sent to all members whether entitled to vote or not and to any debenture holder (see s.5(2) of the Act). Since a special resolution is proposed, 21 clear days' notice of the meeting must be given. However, if the members agree and sign a consent to short notice (see **8.6.1**) the meeting may be held at less than 21 days' notice.

4. The copy special resolution (see **8.10** for form) should be signed by the chairman and filed with the Registrar within 15 days of its being passed.

5. Once 21 days have elapsed from the date of the passing of the resolution, and if no application has been made to the court for the alteration to be cancelled, a reprinted copy of the memorandum, as altered, should be filed with the Registrar (within 15 days of the end of such 21 day period).

NOTICE CONVENING EXTRAORDINARY GENERAL MEETING TO ALTER OBJECTS

LIMITED

NOTICE IS HEREBY GIVEN that an extraordinary general meeting of the above-named company will be held at   on   19   , at   a.m./p.m. for the purpose of considering and, if thought fit, passing the following resolution which will be proposed as a special resolution:

SPECIAL RESOLUTION

That clause 3 of the memorandum of association of the company be altered by the deletion of sub-clause (a) and the substitution of the following new sub-clause (a):

'(a)

,

BY ORDER OF THE BOARD

Secretary

Dated

Registered office

Note: A member entitled to attend and vote at the meeting is entitled to appoint a proxy to attend and vote instead of him. A proxy need not be a member of the company.

NOTES ON 1.15 AND RESOLUTION 2 OF 1.16

The articles of association may be altered, or an entirely new set adopted, by special resolution and the following procedure should be observed:

1. A board meeting should be held to convene an extraordinary general meeting to consider the special resolution (see **7.1.26** for board minute).

2. If it is intended merely to alter the articles, the resolution proposed should be in the form of **1.15** and this will set out the textual amendment in the notice. If an entirely new set of articles is to be adopted the resolution proposed should be in the form of resolution 2 of **1.16** and the revised articles should be attached to the notice or be available for inspection at the registered office of the company during the period from the date of the notice to the date of the meeting.

3. Notice of the meeting must be given to the members entitled thereto (see regulation 38 of Table A and the company's articles of association) and on the company's auditors. Since a special resolution is proposed, 21 clear days' notice of the meeting must be given. However, if the members agree and sign a consent to short notice (see **8.6.1**) the meeting may be held at less than 21 days' notice.

4. The copy special resolution (see **8.10** for form) should be signed by the chairman and filed with the Registrar within 15 days of its being passed along with a reprinted copy of the articles of association (s.18).

NOTICE CONVENING EXTRAORDINARY GENERAL MEETING TO ALTER ARTICLES

LIMITED

NOTICE IS HEREBY GIVEN that an extraordinary general meeting of the above-named company will be held at   on
             19   , at   a.m./p.m. for the purpose of considering and, if thought fit, passing the following resolutions which will be proposed as special resolutions:

SPECIAL RESOLUTIONS

1.   That the articles of association be altered by the insertion of the following new article   :

and that articles   to   be re-numbered accordingly.

2.   That the articles of association be altered by the deletion therefrom of article   and the substitution therefor of the following new article   :

BY ORDER OF THE BOARD

Secretary

Dated

Registered office

Note: A member entitled to attend and vote at the meeting is entitled to appoint a proxy to attend and vote instead of him. A proxy need not be a member of the company.

FOR NOTES TO 1.16 SEE PAGES 42 AND 44

NOTICE CONVENING EXTRAORDINARY GENERAL MEETING TO ADOPT NEW OBJECTS AND NEW ARTICLES

LIMITED

NOTICE IS HEREBY GIVEN that an extraordinary general meeting of the above-named company will be held at   on
            19   , at   a.m./p.m. for the purpose of considering and, if thought fit, passing the following resolutions which will be proposed as special resolutions:

SPECIAL RESOLUTIONS

1.   THAT the provisions of the memorandum of association of the company be altered by the deletion therefrom of clause 3 and the substitution therefor of new clause 3 as set forth in the printed document produced to this meeting and signed by the chairman thereof.

2.   THAT the regulations contained in the printed document produced to this meeting and signed by the chairman thereof be approved and adopted as the articles of association of the company in substitution for and to the exclusion of all the existing articles thereof.

BY ORDER OF THE BOARD

Secretary

Dated

Registered office

Notes: A member entitled to attend and vote at the meeting is entitled to appoint a proxy to attend and vote instead of him. A proxy need not be a member of the company.
Copies of the existing and proposed memorandum and articles of association will be available for inspection at the registered office from the date of this notice and at the meeting itself.

2 Classes of shares

CONTENTS

NOTES ON 2.1

Preference shares usually carry preferential rights as to dividend and/or capital. They do not normally have voting rights, or alternatively have very restricted rights as to voting.

The rights attaching to such shares must be set out in the articles of association or in a special resolution. It is preferable to contain such rights in the articles of association, although this would necessitate a reprint of the articles in accordance with s.18 of the Act.

The preference shares in **2.1** are in a very simple form and give the holders a preferential right to a fixed cumulative dividend. They also give the holders the right to a return of capital on a winding up in priority to any other class of share. It will be noted that the holders only have the right to attend and vote at meetings in certain circumstances.

Preference shares are often issued to shareholders who wish to give financial backing to a company but do not wish to be involved in its day to day running.

The rights attaching to preference shares are a matter of construction of the provision or article creating them and it is therefore important to ensure that the rights are clearly set out. It is therefore advisable to obtain legal advice on the creation of such shares.

PREFERENCE SHARES

The preference shares shall entitle the holders to a fixed cumulative preferential dividend at the rate of   per cent on the capital paid up thereon. The dividend shall rank for payment in priority to the payment of a dividend on any other shares and shall be payable annually on

The preference shares shall entitle the holders thereof on a winding up or other repayment of capital in priority to any other class of shares, to a return of the capital paid up thereon together with a sum equal to any arrears or deficiency of the fixed cumulative preferential dividend calculated down to the date of repayment, whether such dividend shall have been declared or earned.

The preference shares shall not confer on the holders any further rights to participate in the profits or assets of the company.

The preference shares shall not entitle the holders to receive notice of or to attend or vote at any general meeting of the company unless either:

1. at the date of the notice convening the meeting the dividend on the preference shares is   months in arrears; or

2. the business of the meeting includes the consideration of a resolution for the winding up of the company or reducing its capital or the sale of the undertaking of the company or if any resolution directly modifies or abrogates any of the special rights or privileges attached to the preference shares, in which case the holders of the preference shares shall be entitled to vote on any such resolution or resolutions and shall be entitled on a show of hands to one vote and on a poll to one vote for every preference share held.

NOTES ON 2.2

The clause contained in **2.2** should be used in addition to the other rights attaching to the preference shares (see **2.1** for example).

Usually ordinary shares are more valuable than preference shares and convertible preference shares may be an added inducement to investors since they enable such holders to convert their shares into ordinary shares either in certain circumstances, or as in **2.2** at the option of the majority of such shareholders. Such a right therefore increases the value of such shares.

CONVERTIBLE SHARES

The holder or holders of the preference shares shall be entitled at any time to convert the whole or any part of the preference shares into ordinary shares and the following provisions shall have effect:

1. Such conversion shall be effected by notice in writing signed by the holder or holders of the majority of the preference shares given to the company.

2. Conversion of the preference shares into ordinary shares shall take effect immediately upon the delivery of the notice in writing to the company.

3. The ordinary shares resulting from the conversion shall rank *pari passu* in all respects with the existing ordinary shares in the capital of the company.

NOTES ON 2.3

The Companies Act 1981 (now consolidated into the 1985 Act) for the first time enabled a company to issue redeemable shares of any class and further to issue shares redeemable at the option of the company and the shareholder. Prior to the 1981 Act a company could only issue redeemable preference shares to be redeemed at the option of the company.

Redeemable shares enable capital to be returned to the shareholder. The rules concerning redemption of shares are complex and are contained in Part V, Chapter VII of the Act. The following is a very brief summary:

1.   Power to issue such shares must be contained in the company's articles (see regulation 3 of Table A).

2.   The company must have at least two shares which are irredeemable.

3.   The company may only redeem fully paid redeemable shares.

4.   The rights attaching to such shares must be contained in the company's articles.

5.   Shares may be issued with a fixed date for redemption or may be redeemable at the option of the company or the holder.

6.   It is not possible to convert shares into redeemable shares; they must be issued as redeemable shares in the first instance.

7.   Upon redemption form 122 must be filed with the Registrar within one month of the redemption. The issued share capital is reduced by the number of shares redeemed, but the authorised share capital remains the same.

REDEEMABLE ORDINARY SHARES

Subject to Part V, Chapter VII Companies Act 1985, the company may redeem at par all or any of the fully paid redeemable ordinary shares upon giving to the shareholders whose shares are to be redeemed not less than   months' written notice (hereinafter called 'the redemption notice'). In the event of a redemption of part only of the redeemable ordinary shares, the redeemable ordinary shares shall be redeemed pro rata to holdings at the date of the redemption notice or as selected by means of drawings as the directors may determine.

The redemption notice shall fix the time and place for such redemption and shall specify the shares to be redeemed. At the time and place so fixed the holders of the redeemable ordinary shares to be redeemed shall deliver to the company the certificates for such shares for cancellation. The company shall thereupon pay to such holders the amount due on redemption.

The holder or holders of any redeemable ordinary shares may, at any time after   19   call upon the company by notice in writing (hereinafter called 'the shareholders' redemption notice') to redeem such shares comprised in the shareholders' redemption notice. The company shall within three months of the date of such notice, or as soon thereafter as the company can comply with the provisions of the Companies Act 1985, redeem all the shares comprised in such notice.

NOTES ON 2.4

Deferred shares usually provide that the right to dividends or return of capital is deferred to all other classes of shares. They are often convertible into ordinary shares after a number of years as is the case in **2.4**. Such shares are sometimes issued to the children of the member of a small family company and are convertible once the children reach maturity in, for example, 10 to 12 years after issue. Taxation advice should be sought prior to the issue of such shares.

DEFERRED SHARES

Until   the deferred shares shall not entitle the holder
or holders thereof:

1.   to receive any dividend or participate in any profits or surplus assets of the
     company except to receive repayment of capital paid up upon such shares *pari
     passu* with the holder or holders of the ordinary shares in the event of a winding
     up of the company;

2.   to receive notice of nor attend and vote at any general meeting of the company;

but with effect from and including   the deferred
shares and the ordinary shares shall rank *pari passu* in all respects.

NOTES ON 2.5 AND 2.6

2.5 and **2.6** are examples of ordinary and preference share certificates. The Act provides that certificates must be completed and ready for delivery within two months after allotment or after a transfer of shares is lodged (s.185).

A company's articles of association normally give the member the right to receive a share certificate free of charge (see regulation 6 of Table A).

The Act does not dictate the form of a share certificate but s.186 provides that a certificate under the common seal of the company specifying any shares held by a member, is *prima facie* evidence of the title of the member to the shares.

ORDINARY SHARE CERTIFICATES

No. of certificate .... For .... shares

of ....

Nos .... to ....

Dated .... 19 ....

Issued to ....

Folio in register ....

No. of certifcate ....

No. of shares ....

ORDINARY SHARES

.... LIMITED

This is to Certify that .... of ....

.... is/are the registered holder(s) of .... ordinary

shares of £ .... each, in the above-named Company, numbered from .... to ....

inclusive subject to the memorandum and articles of association of the Company, and that upon

each of such shares the sum of £ .... has been paid.

Given under the Common Seal of the said Company

this .... day of .... 19 ....

.... DIRECTOR

.... SECRETARY

FOR NOTES TO 2.6 SEE PAGE 58

PREFERENCE SHARE CERTIFICATES

No. of certificate ....

For .... shares

Nos .... to .... shares

of ....

Issued to ....

Dated .... 19 ....

Folio in register ....

No. of certificate ....

No. of shares ....

PREFERENCE SHARES

.... LIMITED

This is to Certify that ....

.... is/are the registered holder(s) of .... preference

shares of £ .... each, in the above-named Company, numbered from .... to ....

inclusive subject to the memorandum and articles of association of the Company, and that upon

each of such shares the sum of £ .... has been paid.

Given under the Common Seal of the said Company

this .... day of .... 19 ....

.... DIRECTOR

.... SECRETARY

NO TRANSFER OF ANY OF THE ABOVE-MENTIONED SHARES WILL BE REGISTERED UNLESS ACCOMPANIED BY THIS CERTIFICATE.

3 Share capital

CONTENTS

NOTES ON 3.1 AND 3.2

Unless the articles provide otherwise, an ordinary resolution is required to increase share capital and the following procedure should be adopted:

1. At a board meeting the directors should resolve to convene an extraordinary general meeting to pass an ordinary resolution to increase share capital. It is advisable also to propose a resolution authorising the directors to allot relevant securities pursuant to s.80 of the Act (see resolution 2 of **3.2**).

2. The Notice convening the extraordinary general meeting should be served on all the members entitled thereto (see regulation 38 of Table A and the company's articles of association) and on the company's auditors. Since ordinary resolutions are proposed, 14 clear days' notice of the meeting must be given. However, if the members agree and sign a consent to short notice (see **8.6.3**) the meeting may be held at less than 14 days' notice.

3. If it is intended to allot further shares immediately following the extraordinary general meeting to certain shareholders, but not to all, it should be checked that the statutory pre-emption provisions contained in sections 89 and 90 of the Act have been waived (see article 2(d) of **1.2**). If these have not been waived an additional resolution should be proposed as follows:

    'In accordance with section 95 of the Companies Act 1985, the provisions of section 89(1) shall not apply to the Company.'

    Such a resolution must be proposed as a special resolution and therefore 21 clear days' notice is required.

4. Copy resolutions should be available for signing by the chairman and filing with the Registrar. Even though the resolutions in **3.2** are ordinary resolutions, both must be filed with the Registrar within 15 days of the passing of the resolutions, together with form 123.

5. A revised memorandum of association may also be filed but this does not appear to be obligatory under s.18 of the Act.

BOARD MINUTES PRIOR TO INCREASE IN SHARE CAPITAL

LIMITED

Minutes of a meeting of the board of directors held at
at   a.m./p.m. on   19

Present:

(Chairman)

In attendance:

1. It was resolved to convene an extraordinary general meeting of the company at which the following resolutions would be proposed:

    (a) to increase the share capital of the company;

    (b) to authorise the directors to allot shares pursuant to section 80 of the Companies Act 1985.

    The notice of meeting was approved and signed by the secretary on behalf of the board.

2. The secretary was instructed to give the notice to the members of the company entitled thereto and to the company's auditors.

3. It was resolved that the members be requested to agree to holding the meeting on short notice.

4. There being no further business the meeting terminated.

Chairman

FOR NOTES TO 3.2 SEE PAGE 64

NOTICE CONVENING EXTRAORDINARY GENERAL MEETING TO INCREASE SHARE CAPITAL

LIMITED

NOTICE IS HEREBY GIVEN that an extraordinary general meeting of the above-named company will be held at   on
           19   at   a.m./p.m. for the purpose of considering and, if thought fit, passing the following resolutions which will be proposed as ordinary resolutions:

1. THAT the authorised share capital of the company be increased from £   to £   by the creation of   shares of £1 each ranking *pari passu* in all respects with the existing shares in the capital of the company.

2. THAT with effect from the time of the passing of this resolution the directors be unconditionally authorised pursuant to section 80, Companies Act 1985, to allot relevant securities (as defined in that Act) up to the amount of the authorised share capital of the company at the time of the passing of this resolution at any time or times during the period of five years from the date hereof and at any time thereafter pursuant to any offer or agreement made by the company before the expiry of this authority.

BY ORDER OF THE BOARD

Secretary

Dated

Registered office

Note: A member entitled to attend and vote at the meeting is entitled to appoint a proxy to vote instead of him. A proxy need not be a member of the company.

NOTES ON 3.3 AND 3.4

Following the extraordinary general meeting increasing the share capital etc., a further board meeting should be held noting the passing of the various resolutions in the form set out in **3.3**.

These minutes also deal with an allotment of shares. However, prior to any allotment, the articles of association should be checked in order to ascertain whether these contain any pre-emption provisions or whether the statutory pre-emption provisions apply (ss.89 and 90).

The following is a brief summary of the procedure on allotment:

1. On receipt of the application form (see **3.4**) and remittance the share certificates should be prepared (see **2.5** and **2.6**).

2. The directors should pass a resolution allotting the shares (see **3.3**) and the share certificate(s) should be sealed and issued to the allottee(s).

3. The requisite entries should be made in the register of members.

4. Within one month of the date of allotment form PUC2 should be filed with the Registrar, providing the allotment has been made for a cash consideration.

BOARD MINUTES ALLOTTING SHARES

LIMITED

Minutes of a meeting of the board of directors held at

at   a.m./p.m. on   19

Present:

(Chairman)

In attendance:

1. The secretary reported that at an extraordinary general meeting held on   19   ordinary resolutions had been passed increasing the authorised share capital and authorising the directors to allot shares.

2. A form of application from   applying for   shares of £1 each was produced and the receipt of £   , being payment in full therefor, was reported.

3. It was resolved that   shares of £1 each, fully paid be allotted to   .

4. It was resolved that the sealing and issue of share certificate no. for   shares of £1 each, fully paid, in respect of the said allotment, be authorised.

5. There being no further business the meeting terminated.

Chairman

FOR NOTES TO 3.4 SEE PAGE 68

FOR NOTES TO 3.4 SEE PAGE 68

FORM OF APPLICATION FOR SHARES

LIMITED

I enclose a cheque for £   , being payment in full for   shares of £1 each in the above company, and I hereby apply for and request you to allot such shares to me.

   I agree to take the said shares subject to the memorandum and articles of association of the company and I authorise you to enter my name in the register of members as the holder of the said shares.

Dated   19

Signature

Name in full

Address

NOTES ON 3.5

3.5 sets out various resolutions altering the share capital of a company pursuant to s.121. Each of these resolutions must be passed by the company in general meeting, and unless the articles provide otherwise they may be proposed as ordinary resolutions. It will therefore be necessary to give the members fourteen clear days' notice of the meeting. For notice of the extraordinary general meeting and consent to short notice see **8.3** and **8.6.3**.

Consolidation of shares

Providing the articles of association so permit, the shares in a company can be consolidated into shares of a larger nominal value than those into which the capital is currently divided.

Subdivision of shares

If the articles of association so permit, the shares of a company may be subdivided by ordinary resolution into shares of smaller nominal amount, the proportion between the amount paid and any amount unpaid on each subdivided share to remain the same after subdivision as before.

Cancellation of shares

If the articles of association so permit, unissued shares may be cancelled.

Providing the resolution(s) proposed in connection with the above are ordinary resolution(s), it is not necessary to file a copy of the resolutions with the Registrar. However, form 122 must be filed within one month of the date of the passing of the resolution (see s.122).

RESOLUTIONS ALTERING SHARE CAPITAL

CONSOLIDATION

ORDINARY RESOLUTION

THAT the 10,000 shares of 25 pence each in the capital of the company be consolidated and divided into 2,500 shares of £1 each.

SUB-DIVISION

ORDINARY RESOLUTION

THAT the 5,000 shares of £1 each in the capital of the company be sub-divided into 20,000 shares of 25 pence each.

CONVERSION OF SHARES INTO STOCK

ORDINARY RESOLUTION

THAT the 5,000 issued and fully paid shares of £1 each in the capital of the company be converted into £5,000 of stock, transferable in units of 25 pence.

RE-CONVERSION OF STOCK INTO SHARES

ORDINARY RESOLUTION

THAT the £2,000 of stock in the company be reconverted into 8,000 fully paid shares of 25 pence each.

CANCELLATION OF UNISSUED SHARES

ORDINARY RESOLUTION

THAT the 1,000 shares of £1 each in the capital of the company which have not been taken or agreed to be taken by any person be cancelled and that the share capital of the company be diminished by £1,000.

NOTES ON 3.6

If the articles so permit, the capital of the company may be reduced by special resolution and subject to confirmation by the court.

Since an application to the court is required the company's legal advisers should be instructed.

A detailed record should be kept of each stage of the procedure as the secretary will be required to make an affidavit confirming that the appropriate procedural steps have been carried out, e.g. the due calling of the required extraordinary general meeting including the number of notices despatched and the time, date and place of posting.

When the reduction is confirmed by the court, a copy of the relevant order and an approved minute showing the amount of the reduced capital with its division into shares must be filed with the Registrar and the reduction takes effect from the date of such registration. The order should be accompanied by a copy of the memorandum as altered.

RESOLUTION REDUCING CAPITAL

SPECIAL RESOLUTION

THAT the capital of the company be reduced from £10,000 divided into 10,000 shares of £1 each (which have been issued and are fully paid up) to £5,000 divided into 10,000 shares of 50 pence each and that such reduction be effected by returning to the holders of the said shares paid-up capital to the extent of 50 pence per share and by reducing the nominal amount of each of the said shares from £1 to 50 pence.

NOTES ON 3.7, 3.8, 3.9, 3.10, 3.11 AND 3.12

These precedents contain a number of documents dealing with a capitalisation issue (bonus issue). A capitalisation issue involves a capitalisation of reserves and the issue of fully paid shares or debentures.

Prior to effecting a capitalisation issue the following matters should be checked:

1. That the company has sufficient reserves available for capitalisation.

2. That the company has the requisite authority to effect a capitalisation issue (see regulation 110 of Table A). If the company does not have the power to capitalise reserves the articles of association should be altered by including a provision similar to regulation 110. This requires a special resolution and a copy of the same must be filed at the Registry within 15 days of being passed (see **8.10** for form).

3. That the company has sufficient authorised and unissued shares to allot the bonus shares and that the directors are authorised to allot shares pursuant to s.80. If not, ordinary resolutions should be proposed increasing the share capital and authorising the directors to allot shares prior to the capitalisation issue resolution (see **3.2**). Copies of the same must be filed with the Registrar within 15 days of being passed along with form 123.

Once the above matters have been checked a board meeting can be held (see **3.7**). **3.7** will require alteration if, for example, the share capital of the company has to be increased prior to the capitalisation issue.

Provided only ordinary resolutions are to be proposed at the extraordinary general meeting, only fourteen clear days' notice is required. Notice of meeting must be served on the members entitled thereto (see regulation 38 of Table A and the company's articles of association) and on the company's auditors (see **3.8**). If the requisite proportion of members agree, the meeting can be held on short notice (see **8.6.3**). Following the extraordinary general meeting, a further board meeting should be held to note the passing of the resolution(s) (see **3.9**). At this meeting the bonus shares should be allotted and, if required, the renounceable letters of allotment (see **3.10** and **3.11**) can be completed and despatched.

After the date specified in **3.10** has elapsed a further board meeting should be held to issue the bonus shares and instruct the secretary to issue share certificates and record the names of the allottees in the register of members.

Provided an ordinary resolution is passed it is not necessary to file a copy with the Registrar.

Forms 88(2) and 88(3) must be filed within one month of the date of allotment of shares. If shares are renounced, the names of the renouncees should be inserted on the reverse of form 88(2) and not those of the original allottees.

If shares are renounced the provisions of Part IV Finance Act 1986 should be noted since stamp duty reserve tax may be payable.

BOARD MINUTES RECOMMENDING A BONUS ISSUE

                                             LIMITED

Minutes of a meeting of the board of directors held at
                        at   a.m./p.m. on   19

Present:
                                                    (Chairman)

In attendance:

1. It was resolved that the company effect a capitalisation issue to its ordinary shareholders.

2. It was noted that the company had the requisite power to do so pursuant to regulation 110 of Table A, which regulation is included in the company's articles of association.

3. It was noted that the company had sufficient reserves available for capitalisation.

4. It was noted that the company had sufficient authorised but unissued shares and that the directors were duly authorised to allot shares pursuant to section 80 Companies Act 1985.

5. It was thereupon resolved to convene an extraordinary general meeting at which a resolution would be proposed to declare a bonus issue of   ordinary shares for every   ordinary share(s) already held.

6. The notice of meeting was approved and was signed on behalf of the board by the secretary who was instructed to give it to the members of the company entitled thereto and to the company's auditors.

7. It was resolved that the members be requested to agree to holding the meeting on short notice.

8. There being no further business the meeting terminated.

Chairman

FOR NOTES TO 3.8 SEE PAGE 76

NOTICE CONVENING EXTRAORDINARY GENERAL MEETING TO EFFECT BONUS ISSUE

LIMITED

NOTICE IS HEREBY GIVEN that an extraordinary general meeting of the above-named company will be held at   on   19   at   a.m./p.m. for the purpose of considering and, if thought fit, passing the following resolution which will be proposed as an ordinary resolution:

THAT, upon the recommendation of the directors, it is desirable to capitalise the sum of £   (being part of the amount standing to the credit of the company's capital reserve account) and that such sum be capitalised and accordingly the directors be and they are hereby authorised and directed to appropriate the said sum to the holders of the ordinary shares in the capital of the company registered at the close of business on   19   , and to apply such sum in paying up in full at par on behalf of such holders   ordinary share(s) of £1 each (ranking *pari passu* in all respects with the existing ordinary shares of the company save that they will not participate in any dividend to be declared in respect of the year ended   19   ) and that such shares be allotted and distributed credited as fully paid to and among the holders in the proportion of   of the said ordinary shares for every   ordinary share(s) then held, and so that the directors shall have full power to do such acts and things required to give effect to the said capitalisation, allotment and distribution.

BY ORDER OF THE BOARD

Secretary

Dated

Registered office

Note: A member entitled to attend and vote at the meeting is entitled to appoint a proxy to vote instead of him. A proxy need not be a member of the company.

FOR NOTES TO 3.9 SEE PAGE 76

BOARD MINUTES FOLLOWING EXTRAORDINARY GENERAL MEETING AND ALLOTTING BONUS SHARES

LIMITED

Minutes of a meeting of the board of directors held at
at   a.m./p.m. on   19

Present:

(Chairman)

In attendance:

1.   The secretary reported that at an extraordinary general meeting held on   an ordinary resolution had been passed authorising the directors to effect a capitalisation issue.

2.   It was resolved that:

(a)   pursuant to the authority given by and the directions contained in the abovementioned resolution the sum of £   therein referred to be capitalised and appropriated as therein set out.

(b)   ordinary shares of £1 each credited as fully paid up be allotted to the persons and in the amounts set out below.

Name of Shareholder   No. of Shares

(c)   The secretary was instructed to prepare and issue renounceable letters of allotment.

3.   There being no further business the meeting terminated.

Chairman

FOR NOTES TO 3.10 SEE PAGE 76

FULLY PAID LETTER OF ALLOTMENT

LIMITED

FULLY PAID LETTER OF ALLOTMENT

Dated

Dear Sir/Madam,

I am writing to inform you that you have been allotted   ordinary shares of £1 each in the capital of the company. Pursuant to an ordinary resolution passed on the   day of   19   these shares are credited as fully paid and will rank *pari passu* with the other existing ordinary shares in the capital of the company.

If you wish to retain all the shares comprised herein you need do nothing with this letter of allotment. If you wish to dispose of all the shares comprised in this letter, you should complete the letter of renunciation attached hereto and hand this letter to the renouncee before the   day of   19   .

The registration application form, also attached hereto, must be completed and signed by the renouncee (if any) and returned with this letter to the registered office not later than the   day of   19   , to be exchanged for a share certificate.

Unless this letter is returned, duly renounced, on the   day of 19   , the certificate for the shares will be automatically issued in your name.

Yours faithfully,

Secretary

LETTER OF RENUNCIATION AND REGISTRATION APPLICATION FORM

LETTER OF RENUNCIATION

TO THE DIRECTORS OF   LIMITED

I/We hereby renounce my/our right to all the shares specified in the letter of allotment in favour of the person(s) signing the registration application form below.

Dated this   day of   19   .

Signed

REGISTRATION APPLICATION FORM

TO THE DIRECTORS OF   LIMITED

I/We accept the ordinary shares of £   each in the above-named company renounced by the letter of renunciation and I/we request registration in the undermentioned names and in the amounts indicated below, subject to the memorandum and articles of association.

Signed

Name

Address

No. of shares

FOR NOTES TO 3.12 SEE PAGE 76

BOARD MINUTES ISSUING BONUS SHARES AND SHARE CERTIFICATES

LIMITED

Minutes of a meeting of the board of directors held at
              at   a.m./p.m. on   19

Present:

                                  (Chairman)

In attendance:

1. The secretary reported that   letters of renunciation and registration application forms had been received and that the undermentioned shareholders wished to renounce their entitlement in favour of the undermentioned renouncees:

    Name of shareholder   Name of renouncee

2. It was resolved to approve the renunciations and the secretary was thereupon instructed to issue share certificates under the common seal of the company as follows:

    Name of allottee/renouncee   No. of shares

3. The secretary was instructed to register the allottees/renouncees as appropriate in the register of members.

4. The secretary was instructed to file forms 88(2) and 88(3) with the Registrar.

5. There being no further business the meeting terminated.

Chairman

NOTES ON 3.13

3.13 contains a summary of the filing requirements on matters relating to share capital. It specifies the forms which must be filed at the Registry and the time period within which the documents must be submitted.

SUMMARY OF FILING REQUIREMENTS RELATING TO SHARE CAPITAL

Matter	Document(s)	Time Limit
Payment up of partly or nil paid shares	PUC5	within one month of payment
Issue of shares for cash	PUC2	within one month of allotment
Issue of shares for consideration other than cash	PUC3 and contract or, if no contract, Form 88(3)	within one month of allotment
Bonus issue of shares (capitalisation issue)	Form 88(2) and contract or, if no contract, form 88(3)	within one month of allotment
Increase in share capital	Form 123 and copy of ordinary resolution	within 15 days of passing resolution
Consolidation/ subdivision/conversion of shares into stock and vice versa; cancellation of unissued shares	Form 122	within one month of resolution
Variation of class rights	Copy of resolution passed and any consents to variation of class rights	within 15 days of resolution or consent
Particulars of share rights not otherwise registrable	Form 128(1)	one month from allotment of the shares
Particulars of variation of rights not otherwise registrable	Form 128(2)	one month from date of variation
Particulars of change of name (reclassification of a class of shares not otherwise registrable)	Form 128(3)	one month from date of change

4 Transfer of shares

CONTENTS

GENERAL NOTES ON TRANSFER OF SHARES

In order to transfer shares, a proper instrument of transfer must be completed and delivered to the company, unless the shares have transmitted by operation of law (s.183). The form of transfer (see **4.6**) is governed by the Stock Transfer Act 1963.

Unless a company's articles of association contain special provisions (for example see **4.2**) a member wishing to dispose of his shares (the transferor) will complete a stock transfer form and will pass this to the purchaser (the transferee) with the share certificates in exchange for the agreed price. The transferee will then enter his name and address as transferee on the transfer, will date it and will have it stamped at an Inland Revenue stamp office. He will then lodge the transfer and share certificates with the company for registration. On receiving such a transfer the following procedure should be adopted:

1. The details of the transferor and the shareholding transferred should be checked with the share certificate lodged and with the register of members.

2. If the company has several classes of shares in issue, it should be checked that the shares transferred are fully and correctly described. If the shares are partly paid (in which event the transfer will need to be executed by both the transferor and the transferee (see regulation 23 of Table A), it should be checked that the amount shown as paid on each share has been correctly entered on the stock transfer form.

3. It should be checked that the share certificate is the original and that no duplicate has subsequently been issued and is still outstanding. If a duplicate is in existence this too should be surrendered to the company prior to registration.

4. It should be checked that the transfer has been duly executed by the transferor or by his attorney and, if the shares are partly paid, by the transferee.

5. The company's records should be checked to ensure that the holding is free from any lien.

6. It should be checked that the instrument has been duly stamped and that the price (if any) indicated by the consideration shown is broadly in line with the company's shares.

7. If the above matters are in order the share certificate(s) should be cancelled and a new certificate should be prepared in the name of the transferee. If only part of the holding covered by the share certificate lodged is being transferred, a balance certificate should be prepared in the name of the transferor.

8. The transfer should be presented for approval at a meeting of the board of directors (see **7.1.15**) and authority should be sought for the new certificate(s) to be sealed (see **7.1.12**). If the company has restrictions on transfer or pre-emption provisions in connection with transfers, it should be checked that the transfer lodged does not contravene any such provisions.

9. It should be checked whether there is any other reason why the transfer should not be registered, e.g. the transferee is known to be an infant (particularly in the case of partly paid shares). If it is desired to refuse to

register a transfer, either under the power given to the directors by regulation 24 of Table A or by the articles of association (see article 4 of **1.2**) a resolution of the directors must be passed (see **7.1.16**). It is not sufficient merely to take no action on a transfer. Notice of such refusal must be given to the proposed transferee within two months of the date on which the transfer was lodged (s.183(5) and (6)).

10. The transfer should be entered in the register of members.

11. The transfer and cancelled share certificate should be filed.

12. A new certificate should be sealed and sent to the transferee and any balance certificate should be sent to the transferor. Certificates should be ready within two months of the date on which the transfer was lodged (s.185) (see **2.5** and **2.6**).

NOTES ON 4.1

This article allows a member to transfer his shares to members of his family as defined by the article. The directors are only able to refuse to register a transfer of shares if the company has a lien on the share or if it is a partly paid share.

If such a clause is inserted into a company's articles, a further provision should be inserted giving the directors the ability to refuse to register a transfer of shares not made pursuant to these provisions.

TRANSFER BETWEEN FAMILY MEMBERS

1. Subject to regulation 24 of Table A, the directors shall not be entitled to refuse to register any transfer of shares made pursuant to paragraph 2 below.

2. (a)   Any share may be transferred by a member to any child or other issue (including a child by adoption), son-in-law, daughter-in-law, father, mother, brother, sister (including a brother or sister of the half blood or related by adoption), nephew, niece, wife, or husband of such member.

    (b)   Any share of a deceased member may be transferred by his or her legal personal representatives to any child or other issue (including a child by adoption), son-in-law, daughter-in-law, father, mother, brother, sister (including a brother or sister of the half blood or related by adoption), nephew, niece, widow or widower of such deceased member.

    (c)   Any share standing in the names of the trustees of the Will of any deceased member may be transferred upon any change of trustees to the trustees for the time being of such Will.

    (d)   Any share may at any time be transferred to any other member of the company.

NOTES ON 4.2

This precedent is an example of an article giving detailed pre-emption provisions to existing members of the company. If any member wishes to transfer shares he must serve notice on the company. The company must then offer such shares to the existing members of the company on a *pro rata* basis. Any member or the directors can call upon the auditors to certify the fair value of such shares. The certified value will be the price at which the shares are offered for sale. If all or any of the shares are accepted by the members, the transferor must transfer such shares to them. If none of the shares are accepted, or if all the shares are not accepted, the transferor can transfer those shares not accepted to whosoever he thinks fit. However, the directors are able to refuse to register such a transfer if they so wish.

The pre-emption provisions also apply upon the death or bankruptcy of a member.

PRE-EMPTION PROVISIONS ON TRANSFER

1. No share shall be transferred unless and until the rights of pre-emption hereinafter conferred shall have been exhausted.

2. Any person proposing to transfer the legal or beneficial interest in any share (hereinafter called 'the proposing transferor') shall give notice in writing to the company (hereinafter called 'the transfer notice') stating the number of shares he desires to transfer and the price per share. The transfer notice shall only relate to one class of shares and shall not be revocable except with the sanction of the directors.

3. The transfer notice shall constitute the company the agent for the proposing transferor for the sale of all or any of the shares comprised in the transfer notice at the price per share specified in the transfer notice or at the fair value fixed by the auditors in accordance with paragraph (4) below.

4. The shares specified in any transfer notice given to the company shall be offered by the company to the members (other than the proposing transferor) as nearly as may be in proportion to the existing number of shares of the same class held by him. Such offer shall be made in writing (hereinafter called 'the offer notice') and shall specify the price per share as stated in the transfer notice. The offer notice shall limit the time within which the same, if not accepted, will be deemed to be declined. If the auditors are requested to certify the fair value of the shares comprised in the transfer notice pursuant to paragraph (5) below such time limit shall be extended to 15 days after the date of the auditors' certification. The offer notice may state that any member who desires shares in excess of his proportion should in his reply state how many excess shares he desires to have; and if all the members do not claim their proportions the unclaimed shares shall be used to satisfy the claims in excess. If any shares shall not be capable without fractions of being offered to the members in proportion to their existing holdings, the same shall be offered to the members, or some of them, in such proportions or in such manner as may be determined by lots drawn in regard thereto, and the lots shall be drawn in such manner as the directors think fit.

5. Any member or director may, within 21 days of the date of the offer notice, call upon the auditor to certify in writing the sum which in his opinion is the fair value of each share, and such sum shall be deemed to be the price per share at which the shares comprised in the transfer notice are offered for sale. In so certifying the auditor shall be considered to be acting as an expert and not as an arbitrator; and accordingly the Arbitration Acts 1950 to 1979 shall not apply.

6. If the company shall within the appropriate period specified in paragraph (5) above find a member or members willing to purchase all or any of the shares comprised in the transfer notice (hereinafter called 'the purchasers') the company shall give notice in writing to the proposing transferor, and he shall be bound upon payment of the fair value to transfer the shares to the purchasers, who shall be bound to complete the purchase within fourteen days from the date of the last-mentioned notice.

7. If in any case the proposing transferor after having become bound as aforesaid makes default in transferring the shares the company may receive the purchase money on his behalf, and may authorise some person to execute a transfer of the shares in the favour of the purchasers, who shall thereupon be registered as the holders of the shares. The receipt of the company for the purchase money shall be a good discharge to the purchasers.

FOR NOTES TO 4.2 SEE PAGE 96

8. If the company shall not serve notice pursuant to paragraph (6) above of if the company has served notice pursuant to paragraph (6) above but all the shares comprised in the transfer notice have not been accepted, the proposing transferor shall at any time within three calendar months be at liberty subject to paragraph (9) below, to transfer the shares comprised in the transfer notice which have not been accepted to any person at a price not lower than the fair value.

9. If any person (other than an existing member) shall become entitled to any shares in the event of the death or bankruptcy of any member he shall within six months serve a transfer notice on the company in respect of all the shares to which such person had become entitled. If such a person fails to give a transfer notice within the time specified in this paragraph the directors may resolve that he be deemed to serve such a transfer notice. Where a transfer notice is given or deemed to be given under this paragraph and no price per share is specified therein, the directors shall call upon the auditor to fix the fair value.

10. The directors may, in their absolute discretion, and without assigning any reason therefor, decline to register any transfer of any share, whether or not it is a fully paid share; and regulation 24 of Table A shall be modified accordingly.

NOTES ON 4.3

This clause may be useful if the company has issued shares to its employees, although it should be noted that it might not be acceptable to the Inland Revenue if the company wished to enter into an approved share option scheme.

This provides that on ceasing to be employed the directors can call upon the ex-employee to transfer his shares. This ensures that an ex-employee no longer has an interest in the company, and can be particularly useful if he has moved to a competitor, for example.

This clause also provides that the directors shall call upon the auditors to fix a fair value upon the shares.

TRANSFER OF SHARES OF EX-EMPLOYEE

1. In the event of any member who is in the employment of the company ceasing from any cause (otherwise than by reason of his death) to be in such employment the directors may at any time within twelve calendar months thereafter serve notice in writing (hereinafter called 'the sale notice') to such member requesting that he transfer all his shares to any person or persons named in the sale notice at the price specified in the sale notice. If default is made in complying with such a request for a period of twenty-one days the person in default shall at the expiration of the said period be deemed to have served the company with a transfer notice.

2. The directors shall within seven days of a sale notice or deemed sale notice call upon the auditor to fix the fair value of the shares comprised in the sale notice or deemed sale notice. In so certifying the auditor shall be considered to be acting as an expert and not as an arbitrator; and accordingly the Arbitration Acts 1950 to 1979 shall not apply.

NOTES ON 4.4

This provision can be inserted into a company's articles if it has company shareholders and enables such shareholders to freely transfer shares between associated companies. It further provides that if such a company ceases to be an associated company of the original transferor then the shares must be transferred to the original transferor.

TRANSFER BETWEEN ASSOCIATED COMPANIES

In the case of a member which is a company, it may transfer all or any of the shares registered in its name to any other company (in these articles referred to as an 'associated company') which is a holding company of that member or which is another subsidiary of such a holding company (the expressions 'subsidiary' and 'holding company' having the meanings given to them respectively in section 736 of the Companies Act 1985) provided that such transferee company shall transfer all such shares to an associated company of such member forthwith upon such transferee company ceasing to be an associated company of the member.

NOTES ON 4.5

The precedents in **4.5** may be required where the beneficial owner of shares prefers not be the registered shareholder. The shares are in these circumstances registered in the name of a nominee. In such a case the company will have no dealings with the beneficial owner but will be required to address all communications to the registered shareholder, the company not being permitted to recognise any trust affecting any of its shares (s.360).

The need for nominee shareholdings also commonly arises in the case of wholly-owned subsidiary companies. Although the whole of the share capital of the subsidiary will be owned by the holding company, the subsidiary company must still have a minimum of two shareholders (s.24). A common arrangement is for one share to be registered jointly in the name of a director and the holding company itself. Such nominees would normally execute the declaration of trust shown in **4.5.1** and should execute a transfer of the share(s) (see **4.6**), the name of the transferee and the date being left blank. Alternatively, the nominee may be asked to execute an extended form of declaration of trust as shown in **4.5.2**. It will be seen that if the extended declaration of trust is executed, directions must be given by the beneficial owner regarding transfers, dividends, votes etc.

Declarations of trust bear a fixed stamp duty of 50 pence.

DECLARATIONS OF TRUST

4.5.1 DECLARATION OF TRUST (SHORT FORM)

I,   of   , hereby declare that the one ordinary share of £1, fully paid, registered in my name in the register of members of   Limited/p.l.c., is held by me as a nominee for   Limited/p.l.c. and that I have no beneficial interest whatsoever in the said share.

Dated this   day of   19   .

(Signature)

4.5.2 DECLARATION OF TRUST (EXTENDED FORM)

By this deed, I,   of   , hereby acknowledge and declare as follows:

1. I hold the stocks and shares specified in the schedule hereto and all dividends and interest accrued or to accrue upon the same, including bonuses, rights and other privileges arising from such stocks and shares or any of them, upon trust for   Limited/p.l.c. of   (hereinafter called 'the company') and its successors in title and hereby agree to transfer, pay and deal with the said stocks and shares and the dividends and interest payable in respect thereof and any bonuses, rights and privileges arising therefrom in such manner as the company shall from time to time direct.

2. At the request of the company, I agree to attend all meetings of stockholders, shareholders or otherwise which I shall be entitled to attend by virtue of being the registered holder of the said stocks and shares or any of them and to vote thereat as the company shall direct, or alternatively to execute all proxies or other documents which shall be necessary or proper to enable the company or its nominees to attend and vote at any such meeting.

3. If any conditional or preferential right to subscribe for shares or securities in any company or any other option shall be offered to me as holder of the said stocks and shares or any of them or otherwise in respect thereof, or if any call shall be made upon any of the said stocks and shares or other payment demanded in respect thereof, then I agree forthwith to give notice of such offer, call or demand to the company and thereafter to act in relation thereto as the company shall direct.

In witness whereof I have hereunto set my hand and seal this   day of   19   .

THE SCHEDULE referred to

1 share of £1, fully paid, in   Limited

Signed, sealed and delivered
by the above-named
          in the
presence of:

(*Witness's signature*)   (*Signature*)

NOTES ON 4.6

4.6 contains a form of transfer of fully paid shares as provided by the Stock Transfer Act 1963. These forms are available from law stationers.

STOCK TRANSFER FORM

STOCK TRANSFER FORM

(Above this line for Registrars only)

Certificate lodged with the Registrar

Consideration Money £ ....

(For completion by the Registrar/Stock Exchange)

Name of Undertaking	
Description of Security	

Number or amount of Shares, Stock or other security and, in figures column only, number and denomination of units, if any.	Words	Figures
		(units of)

Name(s) of registered holder(s) should be given in full; the address should be given where there is only one holder.

If the transfer is not made by the registered holder(s) insert also the name(s) and capacity (e.g. Executor(s)) of the person(s) making the transfer.

In the name(s) of

I/We hereby transfer the above security out of the name(s) aforesaid to the person(s) named below *or to the several persons named in Parts 2* of *Brokers Transfer Forms relating to the above security.*

Delete words in italics except for stock exchange transactions

Signature(s) of transferor(s)

Stamp of Selling Broker(s) or, for transactions which are not stock exchange transactions, of Agent(s), if any, acting for the Transferor(s).

1. ....

2. ....

3. ....

4. ....

Bodies corporate should execute under their common seal.

Date ....

Full name(s) and full postal address(es) (including County or, if applicable, Postal District number) of the person(s) to whom the security is transferred.

Please state title, if any, or whether Mr., Mrs., or Miss.

Please complete in type-writing or in Block Capitals.

I/We request that such entries be made in the register as are necessary to give effect to this transfer.

Stamp of Buying Broker(s) (if any)

Stamp or name and address of person lodging this form (if other than the Buying Broker(s))

FOR NOTES TO 4.6 SEE PAGE 106

FORM OF CERTIFICATE REQUIRED FOR EXEMPTION FROM STAMP DUTY

Instruments of transfer executed on or after 1 May 1987 are exempt from stamp duty when the transaction falls within one of the following categories and will not need to be seen in stamp offices, provided they are certified as below in accordance with the Stamp Duty (Exempt Instruments) Regulations 1987.

a   The vesting of property subject to a trust in the trustees of the trust on the appointment of a new trustee, or in the continuing trustees on the retirement of a trustee.

b   The conveyance or transfer of property the subject of a specific devise or legacy to the beneficiary named in the will (or his nominee).

c   The conveyance or transfer of property which forms part of an intestate's estate to the person entitled on intestacy (or his nominee).

d   The appropriation of property within section 84 (4) of the Finance Act 1985 (death: appropriation in satisfaction of a general legacy of money) or section 84 (5) or (7) of that Act (death: appropriation in satisfaction of any interest of surviving spouse and in Scotland also of any interest of issue).

e   The conveyance or transfer of property which forms part of the residuary estate of a testator to a beneficiary (or his nominee) entitled solely by virtue of his entitlement under the will.

f   The conveyance or transfer of property out of a settlement in or towards satisfaction of a beneficiary's interest, not being an interest acquired for money or money's worth, being a conveyance or transfer constituting a distribution of property in accordance with the provisions of the settlement.

g   The conveyance or transfer of property on and in consideration only of marriage to a party to the marriage (or his nominee) or to trustees to be held on the terms of a settlement made in consideration only of the marriage.

h   The conveyance or transfer of property within section 83 (1) of the Finance Act 1985 (transfers in connection with divorce, etc.).

i   The conveyance or transfer by the liquidator of property which formed part of the assets of the company in liquidation to a shareholder of that company (or his nominee) in or towards satisfaction of the shareholder's rights on a winding-up.

j   The grant in fee simple of an easement in or over land for no consideration in money or money's worth.

k   The grant of a servitude for no consideration in money or money's worth.

l   The conveyance or transfer of property operating as a voluntary disposition inter vivos for no consideration in money or money's worth nor any consideration referred to in section 57 of the Stamp Act 1891 (conveyance in consideration of a debt, etc.).

m   The conveyance or transfer of property by an instrument within section 84 (1) of the Finance Act 1985 (death: varying disposition).

CERTIFICATE

(1) Insert appropriate category

(2) Delete if the certificate is given by the transferor or his solicitor.

I/We hereby certify that this instrument falls within category . . . . . .[1] in the schedule to the Stamp Duty (Exempt Instruments) Regulations 1987.

I/we confirm that I/we have been duly authorised by the transferor to sign this certificate and that the facts of the transaction are within my/our knowledge. (2)

Signature(s) ....   Description ("Transferor", "Solicitor" etc.)...............

Name(s) ....

Address ....

....

Date ....19 ....

NOTES ON 4.7

In the event of a member reporting the loss of a share certificate the following procedure should be adopted:

1. He should be asked to give an indemnity in respect of the issue of a duplicate certificate, the indemnity to carry the guarantee of a bank, insurance company or guarantee society (see **4.7**). Some companies are prepared to dispense with a guarantee if the value of the shares comprised in the lost certificate is very small.

2. On receipt of a satisfactorily completed indemnity, a duplicate certificate, clearly marked as a duplicate, will be prepared and issued on payment of any fee. (Regulation 7 of Table A provides that expenses may be payable, but otherwise certificates will be issued free of charge.)

INDEMNITY FOR LOST CERTIFICATE

INDEMNITY FOR LOST CERTIFICATE

	(Above this line for Registrar's use only)

To the directors of

The original certificate(s) of title relating to the undermentioned securities of the above-named company has/have been lost or destroyed.

Neither the securities nor the certificate(s) of title thereto have been transferred, charged, lent or deposited or dealt with in any manner affecting the absolute title thereto and the person(s) named in the said certificate(s) is/are the person(s) entitled to be on the register in respect of such securities.

I/We request you to issue (a) duplicate certificate(s) of title for such securities and, in consideration of your doing so, undertake [jointly and severally]* to indemnify you and the company against all claims and demands (and any expenses thereof) which may be made against you or the company in consequence of your complying with this request and of the company permitting at any time hereafter a transfer of the said securities, or any part thereof, without the production of the said original certificate(s).

I/We undertake to deliver to the company for cancellation the said original certificate(s) should the same ever be recovered.

[*Applicable only to joint accounts.]

PARTICULARS OF CERTIFICATE(S) LOST OR DESTROYED

Particulars of certificate	Amount and class of securities	In favour of

Dated this   day of   19   .

Signature(s)

† We   hereby
join in the above indemnity and undertaking.
† *Bank, insurance company or guarantee society.*

NOTES ON 4.8

All documents accepted for registration must indicate the shareholding affected, and must include the full name and address of the shareholder as registered. When names on documents are not fully identifiable with the shareholding, a declaration of identity should be obtained.

DECLARATION OF IDENTITY

DECLARATION OF IDENTITY

To the Directors of   Limited

I,
of
hereby declare that I am one and the same person as *
                    of the same address who is registered in the books of your
company as the holder of   stock/shares represented
by certificate(s) nos.   and further I request and authorise
you to enter my full and correct name, viz.:
                    on your company's registers in respect of the above
mentioned stock/shares.

    Signature
    Date

SUPPORTING DECLARATION

I,
of
hereby declare that I have known the above-named
                    for   years and verify that (s)he is one and the
same person as   who has signed the
above declaration.

    Signature
    Description
    Date

For company's use only
Acknowledged
Plate made
Sheet printed
Index printed
Bank

Note: Stock/share certificate(s) **must** be lodged at the company's office with this request.

* If the declaration relates to the identity of a third party (e.g. if given by an executor regarding the identity of the deceased), the form should be suitably adapted.

NOTES ON 4.9 AND 4.10

The title to shares registered in the name of a deceased member can only be established by producing a grant of probate or administration. A company may consider recognising the widow, widower or next of kin as the person entitled to deal with the shares. If the company is prepared to recognise such a person, the share certificate(s), death certificate, statutory declaration (see **4.9**) and indemnity (see **4.10**) from the claimant should be produced.

This procedure should only be accepted where the value of the estate is small.

STATUTORY DECLARATION BY NEXT OF KIN FOR A SMALL ESTATE

I,

of

do solemnly and sincerely declare that:

1. I am the   of   deceased ('the deceased') who died
    intestate on   19   , and that I am the only person entitled to
    the estate of the deceased.

2. The total value of the estate of the deceased in the United Kingdom, which
    includes   shares of   each, fully paid, in
            Limited/p.l.c., does not exceed £   .

3. No inheritance tax is payable in respect of the estate of the deceased.*

4. I do not intend nor, to the best of my knowledge, does any other person intend
    to apply for a grant of administration of the estate of the deceased.

   And I make this solemn declaration conscientiously believing the same to be true
and by virtue of the provisions of the Statutory Declarations Act 1835.

Declared at

the   day of

one thousand nine hundred and

before me

A Commissioner for Oaths†

* Paragraph 3 may be omitted if a letter from the Capital Taxes Office is produced.
† Or notary public or justice of the peace or solicitor having the powers conferred on a
Commissioner for Oaths.

FOR NOTES TO 4.10 SEE PAGE 114

INDEMNITY BY NEXT OF KIN FOR A SMALL ESTATE

The directors,

Limited

In consideration of your company recognising me as the sole administrator of the estate of   deceased ('the deceased') without the production to the company of a grant of administration of the estate of the deceased, I hereby agree to indemnify you and the company from and against all claims, demands, losses, damages, costs, charges and expenses which you or the company in consequence thereof may sustain, incur or be liable for, and I undertake to complete at the request of the company such document or documents as may be necessary to transfer into my name   shares of   each, fully paid, in the company which are registered in the name of the deceased. I further undertake to obtain and produce to the company a grant of administration of the estate of the deceased if so required by the company.

Dated this   day of   19

Signature
Address

5 Re-registration of companies

CONTENTS

GENERAL NOTES ON RE-REGISTRATION OF A PRIVATE COMPANY AS A PUBLIC COMPANY

Action	Notes
1. Before application	
(a) Check that share capital requirements are met:	s.45
(i) nominal value of allotted share capital is not less than authorised minimum	(A)
(ii) each allotted share is at least 25 per cent paid, and any premium due thereon has been received in full	s.45(5) & (6) permit some exceptions
(iii) where shares have been paid up, in part or in full, by an undertaking to perform work or services, such undertaking has been discharged	
(iv) where the consideration for any fully or partly paid-up shares is non-cash (other than as at iii), the undertaking has been discharged or a contract to do so within 5 years of date of allotment exists	
(b) arrange as necessary for any omissions under (a) to be rectified	
(c) check that the relevant balance sheet is accompanied by an unqualified auditors' report	s.43(3)(c) (B)
(d) obtain written statement from the auditors that in their opinion the relevant balance sheet (see (c)) shows that the net assets were not less than the called-up capital and undistributable reserves	s.43(3)(b)
(e) where appropriate, obtain an expert's report on any non-cash consideration received for shares allotted since the relevant balance sheet date	s.44(2)
(f) convene and hold an extraordinary general meeting to pass special resolution that:	
(i) the company be re-registered as a public company	
(ii) the name of the company to be changed to include the suffix 'Public Limited Company' or 'p.l.c.'	(C)
(iii) the memorandum of association be amended to state that the company is a public company and as necessary otherwise to conform to Table F in The Companies (Tables A to F) Regulations 1985	
(iv) if necessary, the articles of association be amended to conform to the requirements of a public company	
(g) statutory declaration on form 43(3)(e) to be made by director or secretary	

Action	Notes
2. Application (a) complete application on form 43(3) and forward to Registrar, accompanied by amended memorandum (and articles) of association and documents at 1(c), 1(d), 1(e) (if applicable) and 1(g) and remittance for the fee of £50 (b) if approved, the Registrar will issue new certificate of incorporation as public company	

3. After approval of application
(a) on receipt of new certificate of incorporation:
  (i) issue amendments to memorandum (and articles) of association to all holders thereof, drawing attention to the company's changed status;
  (ii) amend all stationery, signs, etc., to show new name to conform with ss. 348 and 349;
  (iii) obtain and adopt common seal in new name	

Notes

(A) Authorised minimum at time of going to press (April 1988) is £50,000. This is subject to amendment by Statutory Instrument.

(B) The 'relevant balance sheet' is a balance sheet prepared not more than 7 months before the application.

(C) Sections 25–27 set out in the regulations regarding use of these words and their Welsh equivalents. The Registrar will accept the letters 'p.l.c.' (and its Welsh equivalent) in either lower or upper case and with or without intervening stops.

NOTES ON 5.1, 5.2 AND 5.3

The precedents in **5.1, 5.2** and **5.3** assume that the company already meets the minimum share capital requirements, and that the relevant balance sheet, auditors' report and written statement of auditors are available. (See generally ss. 43 to 47).

It further assumes that the company wishes to adopt entirely new articles and not simply to make alterations to its existing articles. If the articles are only to be altered see **1.15** for the wording, which should replace (b) of **5.2**.

However, if it is necessary to increase the share capital, this resolution along with a resolution to authorise the directors to allot shares pursuant to s.80 should be proposed (see **3.2**) prior to the resolution that the company be re-registered. If it is practical the extraordinary general meeting can be adjourned following the passing of the resolutions dealing with share capital, in order that the additional shares may be allotted. If the additional shares are to be allotted by way of a capitalisation issue, a further resolution should be proposed prior to the resolution to re-register (see **3.8** etc.).

If it is intended to change the name of the company other than by replacing 'Limited' with 'Public Limited Company' or its authorised abbreviation, a resolution should be proposed prior to the resolution to re-register (see **1.12**). This resolution must provide that the company's name ends with the word 'Limited' and not 'Public Limited Company'. If a change of name resolution is proposed, the re-registration is likely to take a little longer and a remittance of £90 should be forwarded to the Registrar (£50 for re-registration and £40 for the change of name).

A board meeting should be held to convene an extraordinary general meeting to consider the special resolution to re-register (see **5.1**).

Notice of meeting (see **5.2**) must be served on the members entitled thereto (see regulation 38 of Table A and the company's articles of association) and on the company's auditors. Since a special resolution is proposed, 21 clear days' notice of the meeting must be given. However, if the members agree and sign a consent to short notice (see **8.6.1**) the meeting may be held at less than 21 days' notice.

The copy special resolution (see **8.10** for form) should be signed by the chairman and filed with the Registrar within 15 days of its being passed together with the documents listed in **5.3**.

BOARD MINUTES PRIOR TO RE-REGISTRATION OF COMPANY AS A PUBLIC COMPANY

LIMITED

Minutes of a meeting of the board of directors held at
at   a.m./p.m. on   19

Present:

(Chairman)

In attendance:

1. It was resolved that the company seek re-registration as a public company pursuant to section 43 of the Companies Act 1985.

2. The secretary confirmed that the company already complied with the minimum share capital requirements for a public company pursuant to section 118 of the Companies Act 1985.

3. It was noted that the memorandum of association need only be altered as specified in section 43 of the Companies Act 1985.

4. It was noted that the opportunity should be taken to update the articles of association to comply with the 1985 Table A and the Companies Act 1985.

5. A notice convening an extraordinary general meeting of the company for   on   19   was produced to the meeting. The extraordinary general meeting was to be convened to propose a resolution that the company be re-registered as a public company.

6. The notice of meeting was approved and signed by the secretary on behalf of the board and the secretary was instructed to serve it on the members entitled thereto and on the company's auditors.

7. There being no further business the meeting terminated.

Chairman

FOR NOTES TO 5.2 SEE PAGE 122

NOTICE CONVENING EXTRAORDINARY GENERAL MEETING TO RE-REGISTER COMPANY AS A PUBLIC COMPANY

LIMITED

NOTICE IS HEREBY GIVEN that an extraordinary general meeting of the above-named company will be held at   on
                    19   at   a.m./p.m. for the purpose of considering and, if thought fit, passing the following resolution which will be proposed as a special resolution:

SPECIAL RESOLUTION

THAT pursuant to the provisions of section 43, Companies Act 1985, the company be re-registered as a public company and

(a) the company's memorandum of association be altered as follows:

    (i) by deleting the existing clause 1 and substituting therefor the following clauses to be numbered 1 and 2:

        '1. The company's name is   Public Limited Company.

        2. The company is to be a public company.'

    (ii) by re-numbering the existing clauses 2, 3, 4 and 5 as clauses 3, 4, 5 and 6 respectively.

(b) the regulations contained in the printed document produced to this meeting and for the purpose of identification signed by the chairman thereof be approved and adopted as the articles of association of the company in substitution for and to the exclusion of all the existing articles thereof.

BY ORDER OF THE BOARD

Secretary

Dated

Registered office

Notes: A member entitled to attend and vote at the meeting is entitled to appoint a proxy to attend and vote instead of him. A proxy need not be a member of the company.
    Copies of the existing and proposed memorandum and articles of association of the company will be available for inspection at the registered office of the company from the date of this notice and will be available at the meeting itself.

FOR NOTES TO 5.3 SEE PAGE 122

BOARD MINUTES FOLLOWING EXTRAORDINARY GENERAL MEETING TO RE-REGISTER COMPANY AS A PUBLIC COMPANY

LIMITED

Minutes of a meeting of the board of directors held at
                    at   a.m./p.m. on   19

Present:

                                                        (Chairman)

In attendance:

1.   It was noted that at an extraordinary general meeting held on
      19   , a special resolution that the company be re-registered as a public
      company was passed.

2.   The secretary thereupon produced the following documents:

      (a)   a certified copy of the special resolution;

      (b)   a printed copy of the memorandum and articles of association as altered,
             duly signed by the chairman of the extraordinary general meeting;

      (c)   an application form – form 43(3);

      (d)   statutory declaration – form 43(3)(e);

      (e)   copy of the 'relevant balance sheet' and the auditors' unqualified report
             thereon;

      (f)   copy of the auditors' written statement in accordance with s.43(3)(b);

      (g)   cheque for £50, being the re-registration fees.

3.   It was thereupon resolved that   , a director of the
      company, be authorised to make the declaration on form 43(3)(e) and that he
      complete the application form on form 43(3).

4.   The secretary was instructed to file the documents listed (a) to (g) with the
      Registrar.

5.   There being no further business the meeting terminated.

Chairman

GENERAL NOTES ON RE-REGISTRATION OF A PUBLIC COMPANY AS A PRIVATE COMPANY

Action	Notes

1. Before application
(a) Convene and hold an extraordinary general meeting to pass special resolution that:
   (i) the company be re-registered as a private company (see **5.4**)
   (ii) the name of the company be changed by substituting 'Limited' for 'Public Limited Company' or 'p.l.c.'
   (iii) the memorandum of association (and articles if necessary) be amended as necessary to delete any reference to public company status
	s.10

2. Application (a) complete application on form 53 and forward to the Registrar, accompanied by copy of special resolution at 1(a) and amended memorandum (and articles) of association (b) notify Registrar immediately on form 54 of any shareholders' application under s.54 for cancellation of special resolution (c) If 2(b) applies, forward to the Registrar copy of the resulting court order within 15 days of its issue (d) if no application under s.54 is made within 28 days of passing of special resolution, or, if so, the court order confirms the special resolution, the Registrar will issue new certificate of incorporation as private company	

3. After approval of application
(a) on receipt of new certificate of incorporation:
   (i) issue amendments to memorandum (and articles) of association to all holders thereof, drawing attention to the company's changed status
   (ii) amend all stationery, signs, etc., to show new name to conform with ss. 348 and 349
   (iii) obtain and adopt common seal in new name	

NOTES ON 5.4

5.4 contains the form of notice convening an extraordinary general meeting that is required if a public company is to be re-registered as a private company (see generally ss. 53 to 55).

See the previous page for the procedure on re-registration.

The copy resolution for filing with the Registrar should be in the form of **8.10**.

NOTICE CONVENING EXTRAORDINARY GENERAL MEETING TO RE-REGISTER PUBLIC COMPANY AS A PRIVATE COMPANY

PUBLIC LIMITED COMPANY

NOTICE IS HEREBY GIVEN that an extraordinary general meeting of the above-named company will be held at   on   19   at   a.m./p.m. for the purpose of considering, and if thought fit, passing the following resolution which will be proposed as a special resolution:

SPECIAL RESOLUTION

THAT the company, being a public company, be re-registered as a private company pursuant to section 53 Companies Act 1985; and

(a)   the company's memorandum be altered as follows:

   (i)   by deleting the existing clause 1 and substituting therefor the following clause 1:
   'The Company's name is   Limited';

   (ii)   by deleting clause 2;

   (iii)   by renumbering the existing clauses 3, 4, 5 and 6 as clauses 2, 3, 4 and 5;

(b)   the regulations contained in the printed document produced to this meeting and for the purpose of identification signed by the chairman thereof be approved and adopted as the articles of association of the company in substitution for and to the exclusion of all the existing articles thereof.

BY ORDER OF THE BOARD

Secretary

Dated

Registered office:

Note: A member entitled to attend and vote at the meeting is entitled to appoint one or more proxies to attend and vote instead of him. A proxy need not also be a member of the company.

Copies of the existing and proposed memorandum and articles of association of the company will be available for inspection at the registered office of the company from the date of this notice and will be available at the meeting itself.

GENERAL NOTES ON RE-REGISTRATION OF A LIMITED COMPANY AS AN UNLIMITED COMPANY

A company limited by shares may be re-registered as an unlimited company pursuant to ss. 49 and 50 provided it has not previously been registered as unlimited. The procedure is as follows:

1. An application is made to the Registrar on form 49(1) which sets out the alterations to the memorandum and articles necessary to make them conform to the requirements for unlimited companies (see Table E in The Companies (Tables A to F) Regulations 1985.

2. The application must be accompanied by a form of assent to the re-registration on form 49(8)(a) signed by or on behalf of every member, a statutory declaration by the directors pursuant to s.49(1)(b) that such assents have been signed by all the members personally or by duly authorised agents (form 49(8)(b)) and a printed copy of the memorandum and articles incorporating the alterations set out in the application.

   It may be convenient to adopt an entirely new set of articles, and if this is desired a special resolution should be passed (see **1.16**). A copy of this resolution must be filed within 15 days of being passed (see **8.10**). If new articles are adopted it is usual to file the resolution along with the above-mentioned documents.

3. A remittance for the fee of £5 should also accompany the application.

4. If the application is accepted, the Registrar issues a new certificate of incorporation on re-registration stating that the company is unlimited and the alterations to the memorandum and articles thereupon take effect.

NOTES ON 5.5, 5.6 AND 5.7

An unlimited company may re-register as limited under ss. 51 and 52 provided it has not previously been registered as limited. The procedure is as follows:

1. A board meeting should be held to convene an extraordinary general meeting to consider the special resolution.

2. Notice of meeting must be served on the members entitled thereto (see regulation 38 of Table A and the company's articles of association) and on the company's auditors. Since the company is an unlimited company only seven days' notice need be given.

3. The special resolution proposed must state the manner in which the members' liability is to be limited and the amount of the share capital and make any necessary alterations to the memorandum and articles to bring them into conformity with the requirements for a limited company (see **5.6**).

4. A copy of the special resolution must be filed with the Registrar within 15 days of being passed (see **8.10**).

5. Application is made to the Registrar on form 51 accompanied by a printed copy of the memorandum and articles (see **1.1** and **1.2**, specimen memorandum and articles for a private company limited by shares).

6. A remittance for the fee of £50 should also accompany the application.

7. Form PUC6 (statement relating to a chargeable transaction of a capital company) must also be filed and it is usual to file this form with the application.

8. If the application is accepted, the Registrar issues a new certificate of incorporation on re-registration stating the new limited status of the company, and the alterations to the memorandum and articles set out in the special resolution thereupon take effect.

BOARD MINUTES PRIOR TO RE-REGISTRATION OF COMPANY AS A LIMITED COMPANY

Minutes of a meeting of the board of directors held at
                                    at   a.m./p.m. on   19

Present:

                                                           (Chairman)

In attendance:

1. It was resolved that the company seek re-registration as a limited company pursuant to section 51 of the Companies Act 1985.

2. It was noted that the only changes necessary to the memorandum of association would be those to be made pursuant to section 51 of the Companies Act 1985.

3. It was resolved that it would be appropriate to adopt new articles of association in the form produced to the meeting.

4. It was thereupon resolved to convene an extraordinary general meeting at which a resolution would be proposed to re-register the company as limited.

5. The notice of meeting was approved and signed by the secretary and the secretary was instructed to serve it on the members of the company entitled thereto and on the company's auditors.

6. There being no further business the meeting terminated.

Chairman

FOR NOTES TO 5.6 SEE PAGE 134

NOTICE CONVENING EXTRAORDINARY GENERAL MEETING TO RE-REGISTER COMPANY AS A LIMITED COMPANY

NOTICE IS HEREBY GIVEN that an extraordinary general meeting of the above-named company will be held at   on   19   at   a.m./p.m. for the purpose of considering and, if thought fit, passing the following resolution which will be proposed as a special resolution:

SPECIAL RESOLUTION

THAT the company be converted from an unlimited company with a share capital to a company limited by shares having an authorised share capital of £   divided into shares of £   each, and

(a) that the company's memorandum of association be altered as follows:

 (i) so that it states that the name of the company is '   Limited';

 (ii) that the following additional clauses be added thereto to be numbered 4 and 5 respectively:

  '4. The liability of the members is limited.

  5. The share capital of the company is £   divided into shares of £   each.'

(b) that the regulations contained in the printed document produced for this meeting and for the purpose of identification signed by the chairman thereof be approved and adopted as the articles of association of the company in substitution for and to the exclusion of all the existing articles thereto.

BY ORDER OF THE BOARD

Secretary

Dated the   day of   19

Registered office

Notes: A member entitled to attend and vote at the above meeting is entitled to appoint a proxy to attend and vote instead of him. A proxy need not be a member of the company.

Copies of the existing and proposed memorandum and articles of association of the company will be available at the registered office of the company from the date of this notice and at the meeting itself.

FOR NOTES TO 5.7 SEE PAGE 134

BOARD MINUTES FOLLOWING EXTRAORDINARY GENERAL MEETING TO RE-REGISTER COMPANY AS A LIMITED COMPANY

Minutes of a meeting of the board of directors held at

                     at   a.m./p.m. on   19

Present:

                                          (Chairman)

In attendance:

1. It was noted that at an extraordinary general meeting of the company held on   19   , a special resolution had been passed that the company be re-registered as a limited company.

2. The following documents were thereupon produced to the meeting:

   (a) the special resolution;

   (b) a reprinted copy of the company's memorandum and articles of association duly signed by the chairman of the meeting;

   (c) form 51;

   (d) form PUC6;

   (e) a cheque in the sum of £50 being the fees on re-registration.

3. The secretary was instructed to file the above-mentioned documents with the Registrar and to order a new company seal once the certificate of incorporation on re-registration has been duly issued.

4. There being no further business the meeting terminated.

Chairman

6 Purchase of own shares

CONTENTS

NOTES ON 6.1, 6.2, 6.3 AND 6.4

The Companies Act 1985 Part V Chapter VII enables a company to purchase its own shares. The procedure is as follows:

1. The articles of association should be checked to ensure the company has the requisite power to purchase its own shares (see regulation 35 of Table A). If it does not have the power, a special resolution should be proposed at the extraordinary general meeting referred to below, altering the articles of association to include a provision in the terms of regulation 35 of Table A.

2. A proposed contract should be agreed between the proposing vendor and the company (see **6.3**).

3. An extraordinary general meeting of the company should be convened to deal with the following matters:

    (a) alteration of articles (if necessary);

    (b) approval of contract of purchase or memorandum of its terms;

    (c) approve payment out of capital (if necessary).

    Since special resolutions are proposed, 21 clear days' notice of the meeting must be given.

4. The members can be asked to agree to the holding of the meeting on short notice (see **8.6**). Even if the members agree to hold the meeting on short notice it will still be necessary to give 15 days' notice of the meeting since a copy of the contract of purchase, or memorandum of its terms, must be available at the registered office of the company for 15 days prior to the date of the meeting (see s.164).

5. The extraordinary general meeting can then be held.

6. A copy of the special resolution(s) in the appropriate form (see **8.10**) should be filed with the Registrar within 15 days of being passed.

7. If the purchase is effected wholly out of distributable profits, the purchase of the shares can proceed immediately following the passing of the resolution and the signing of the contract.

8. Within 28 days of the purchase, form 169 must be filed with the Registrar along with a remittance for stamp duty payable (s.66 Finance Act 1986).

9. The contract of purchase must be retained for ten years after completion of the sale of the shares and must be available for inspection by members during business hours.

10. Following a purchase by a company of its own shares the issued share capital is reduced accordingly, but the authorised share capital remains the same. If it is desired to cancel these unissued shares, an ordinary resolution can be proposed (see **3.5**) and form 122 should be filed within one month of the passing of the resolution.

BOARD MINUTES PRIOR TO EXTRAORDINARY GENERAL MEETING

LIMITED

Minutes of a meeting of the board of directors held at

at,   a.m./p.m. on   19

Present:

(Chairman)

In attendance:

1. The secretary reported that   wished to sell his shares to the company pursuant to the provisions of s.162 Companies Act 1985.

2. The secretary further reported that clearance had been obtained from the Inland Revenue pursuant to s.53 Finance Act 1982 and s.464 Income and Corporation Taxes Act 1970.

3. It was thereupon resolved to convene an extraordinary general meeting to propose a special resolution to approve a proposed contract between the company and   for the purchase by the company of   shares.

4. The notice of meeting was approved and was signed on behalf of the board by the secretary and the secretary was instructed to serve it on the members of the company and on the auditors.

5. It was resolved that the members be requested to agree to holding the meeting on short notice. The provisions of s.164(6) which states that the contract of purchase had to be available for 15 days prior to the date of the meeting, were noted.

6. There being no further business the meeting terminated.

Chairman

FOR NOTES TO 6.2 SEE PAGE 142

NOTICE CONVENING AN EXTRAORDINARY GENERAL MEETING

LIMITED

NOTICE IS HEREBY GIVEN that an extraordinary general meeting of the above-named company will be held at   on
                    19   at   a.m./p.m. for the purpose of considering and, if thought fit, passing the following resolution which will be proposed as a special resolution:

SPECIAL RESOLUTION

THAT the contract proposed to be made between the company and
                    for the purchase of   shares of £   each in the company for £   the terms of which are set out in the copy of the proposed contract produced to this meeting and signed by the chairman for the purpose of identification, be authorised.

BY ORDER OF THE BOARD

Secretary

Dated

Registered office

Notes: A member entitled to attend and vote at the above meeting shall be entitled to appoint a proxy who need not be member of the company to attend and vote instead of him.

A copy of the proposed contract of purchase will be available at the registered office of the company for fifteen days prior to the date of the above meeting and at the meeting.

FOR NOTES TO 6.3 SEE PAGE 142

CONTRACT OF PURCHASE

THIS AGREEMENT is made the   day of
19

BETWEEN

1.   of
    (hereinafter called 'the Vendor')
    and

2.   Limited whose registered office is situate
    at ·
    (hereinafter called 'the company')

WHEREAS

A. The company was incorporated in   on
    19   under the Companies Act(s)
    and has an authorised share capital of   divided into
    shares of   each of which   are in issue and are fully paid

B. The vendor is the beneficial owner of   shares of   each in the
    capital of the company

C. This agreement is made by the company pursuant to Part V of the Companies
    Act 1985 and regulation 35 of Table A, which regulation is embodied in the
    articles of association of the company

D. The terms of this agreement were authorised by a special resolution of the
    company passed on   19

NOW IT IS HEREBY AGREED as follows:

1. The vendor shall sell and the company shall purchase   shares of
        each in the company, which shares are free from all charges, liens,
    encumbrances and claims.

2. The total purchase price for the shares shall be payable in cash on completion.

3. Completion shall take place on
                19   at

    whereupon:
    (a) the vendor shall deliver to the company for cancellation the share
    certificate(s) in respect of the number of shares sold under this agreement or in
    the case of lost certificates such indemnity as the company may reasonably
    require;

    (b) the company shall deliver to the vendor a cheque in the sum of £
    pursuant to clause 2 of this agreement.

4. Time shall be of the essence of this agreement.

5. (a) This agreement constitutes the whole agreement between the parties hereto
    and no variation shall be effective unless made in writing;

    (b) this agreement shall be governed by the law of England/Scotland.

AS WITNESS etc.

FOR NOTES TO 6.4 SEE PAGE 142

BOARD MINUTES FOLLOWING EXTRAORDINARY GENERAL MEETING

                                                    LIMITED

Minutes of a meeting of the board of directors held on the
at   at,   a.m./p.m. on   19

Present:

                                                    (Chairman)

In attendance:

1.   The secretary reported that at an extraordinary general meeting held on
     the   19   a special resolution had been
     passed approving the proposed contract of purchase between the company
     and   .

2.   It was thereupon resolved that   be authorised to execute the
     contract with   on behalf of the company.

3.   The secretary was instructed to file a copy of the special resolution with the
     Registrar together with form 169 and a cheque for £   being the stamp duty
     payable.

4.   The secretary was further instructed to notify the Inland Revenue of the
     purchase immediately after the execution of the contract and to retain the
     contract with the records of the company for ten years.

5.   There being no further business the meeting terminated.

Chairman

NOTES ON 6.5, 6.6 AND 6.7

A private company may, if authorised by its articles (see regulation 35 of Table A) make a payment in respect of the purchase of its own shares otherwise than out of distributable profits or the proceeds of a fresh issue of shares. The payment is known as the 'permissible capital payment'.

It should be noted that a payment out of capital cannot be made until all the company's distributable profits have been utilised.

If the purchase of own shares is to be effected out of capital or partially out of capital, all distributable profits having been utilised, it will be necessary to propose a further special resolution at the extraordinary general meeting (see **6.5**).

Not earlier than the sixth day prior to the date of the meeting all the directors should complete and make a statutory declaration on form 173. The auditors should then provide a report (see **6.6** for an example). This should be attached to form 173.

Within one week of the extraordinary general meeting and passing of the special resolution approving the payment out of capital, the company must publish a suitable notice in the *Gazette* and in a national newspaper (see **6.7**). If preferred, the company can give a similar form of notice to each of its creditors instead of advertising in a national newspaper. However, this would only be practicable if the company had a small number of creditors.

No later than the date upon which the first notice is published in a newspaper or notice given to the creditors, a copy of the statutory declaration and auditors' report must be delivered to the Registrar. The original documents must be retained at the company's registered office throughout the period beginning with the date upon which the first notice is published in a newspaper or given to creditors and ending five weeks after the date of the special resolution approving the permissible capital payment. These documents must be available for inspection during usual business hours during this period.

Not earlier than five nor more than seven weeks after the date of the resolution authorising payment, the sale of the shares can proceed.

Within 28 days of the purchase, form 169 must be filed with the Registrar together with a remittance for the stamp duty payable (s.66 Finance Act 1986).

SPECIAL RESOLUTION APPROVING PAYMENT OUT OF CAPITAL

LIMITED

NOTICE IS HEREBY GIVEN that an extraordinary general meeting of the above-named company will be held at
on   19   , at   a.m./p.m. for the purpose of considering and, if thought fit, passing the following resolution which will be proposed as a special resolution:

SPECIAL RESOLUTION

THAT the payment of £   out of the capital of the company pursuant to sections 171 and 172 Companies Act 1985 in respect of the purchase of shares of £   each, be authorised.

BY ORDER OF THE BOARD

Secretary

Dated

Registered office

Note: A member entitled to attend and vote at the above meeting shall be entitled to appoint a proxy, who need not be a member of the company, to attend and vote instead of him.

FOR NOTES TO 6.6 SEE PAGE 150

AUDITORS' REPORT

Dear Sirs,

In our opinion the amount specified in the statutory declaration attached hereto as the permissible capital payment for the shares to be purchased by the company has been properly determined in accordance with sections 171 and 172 Companies Act 1985.

We are not aware of anything to indicate that the opinion expressed by you in the statutory declaration as to any of the matters referred to in section 173(3) of the aforementioned Act is unreasonable in all the circumstances.

Signed

FOR NOTES TO 6.7 SEE PAGE 150

NOTICE FOR THE *GAZETTE*

LIMITED

Co. No.

NOTICE IS HEREBY GIVEN THAT:

At an extraordinary general meeting of the above company held at
                                        on   19   , a
special resolution was passed authorising the payment of £   out of the capital
of the company in respect of the purchase by the company of   shares of
£   each from   . The amount of the
permissible capital payment was £   .

    The statutory declaration and auditors' report dated
            19   are available for inspection at
                , the registered office of the company.

    Any creditor of the company may apply to the High Court pursuant to section 176
of the Companies Act 1985 within five weeks immediately following the date of the
aforementioned special resolution,   19   for an order
prohibiting the payment,

Dated

Signed

Authenticated for advertising in the *Gazette* by

                                        Chartered Secretary/Solicitor/Accountant

7 Directors, secretary and auditors

CONTENTS

NOTES ON 7.1

The precedents in **7.1** contain a number of resolutions which directors of a company may need to pass during the lifetime of the company. Many of the resolutions are self-explanatory, but the following notes may be of assistance:

7.1.1 – This contains a form for a written directors' resolution. This type of resolution can be useful if the directors have difficulty in meeting. It should be noted that such a resolution must be signed by all the directors of the company entitled to receive notice of a meeting of directors (see regulation 93 of Table A).

7.1.2 – Regulation 89 of Table A fixes the quorum for directors' meetings at two, this resolution may be passed if the directors have power by the articles (as in regulation 89) to alter the quorum.

7.1.4 – The directors are given power to appoint a committee if an article is included in the articles of association similar to regulation 72 of Table A.

7.1.5 – Regulation 79 of Table A empowers the directors to fill a casual vacancy in the board. Form 288 must be filed with the Registrar within 14 days of the appointment.

7.1.6 – See regulation 76 of Table A.

7.1.9 – Section 375 provides for a corporate body which is a shareholder to be physically represented at a company meeting by a person appointed as its representative by a resolution of its directors. This type of representative, in contrast to a proxy not himself a member, is entitled both to speak at a meeting and to vote either on a show of hands or on a poll. Evidence of his appointment in the form of a certified copy of a board minute, or under the seal of the company, should be produced by the representative on entering the meeting, unless it has previously been lodged.

7.1.10 – Form 287 must be filed with the Registrar within 14 days of the resolution.

7.1.12 – Every company should have a common seal. If the seal is only used infrequently, specific reference to documents sealed may be made in the minutes of the meeting of the directors authorising the sealing. Where, however, the seal is frequently used, particulars of documents sealed will normally be entered in a seal book which will be produced at each board meeting and an appropriate confirmatory resolution (as in **7.1.11**) be passed.

7.1.12 – For notes on changing accounting reference date see pages 184–5.

7.1.13 – Each share in a company is required to be distinguished by its appropriate number, but distinguishing numbers may be dispensed with if all the issued shares in the company (of the class concerned) are fully paid up and rank *pari passu* for all purposes (see s.182(2)).

7.1.15 – Refusal to register must be positively effected by a resolution. Notice of refusal to register must be given to the proposed transferee within two months of the date on which the transfer was lodged (see s.183(5)).

7.1.19 – Within one month of the date of allotment, form PUC2 should be filed, since such an allotment is considered to be for a cash consideration (see s.738).

7.1.21, 7.1.22, 7.1.23 and **7.1.24** – Calls on shares arise when under the terms of issue of shares only part of the nominal amount of each share is payable at the

VARIOUS DIRECTORS' RESOLUTIONS

7.1.1 WRITTEN DIRECTORS' RESOLUTION

LIMITED

Pursuant to the authority given by regulation 93 of Table A (which regulation is incorporated in the company's articles of association), we, the undersigned, being all the directors for the time being of the company entitled to receive notice of meetings of the directors resolve:

THAT

Dated

Signed

7.1.2 FIXING A QUORUM

THAT the quorum necessary for the transaction of the business of the directors be fixed at three.

7.1.3 APPOINTMENT OF DIRECTOR BY SOLE CONTINUING DIRECTOR

Pursuant to the authority given by regulation 90 of Table A (which regulation is incorporated in the company's articles of association) I,
the sole continuing director of the company hereby appoint
          to be a director of the company to fill the vacancy caused by the resignation
of   .

Dated

Signed

7.1.4 RESOLUTIONS FOR APPOINTMENT OF COMMITTEE

THAT pursuant to article   of the company's articles of association, any [one] director be appointed a committee to take any actions and to complete all documents necessary to   .

THAT pursuant to article   of the company's articles of association,   and   [any two directors of the company] be appointed a committee with power to approve share transfers and to authorise the sealing and issue of share certificates in respect thereof.

7.1.5 FILLING A CASUAL VACANCY

THAT   be appointed a director of the company in the place of   .   shall hold office until the next annual general meeting.

time of allotment and no dates are fixed for the payment of the balance. The making of calls and forfeiture are governed by the company's articles of association (see regulations 12 to 22 of Table A). If a call remains unpaid the ultimate sanction is forfeiture. The practice on forfeiture must be strictly in accordance with the procedural requirements set out in the articles of association. If a procedure is not adhered to, the forfeiture may be invalid and it may therefore be prudent to take legal advice.

7.1.6 RECOMMENDATION OF DIRECTORS FOR ELECTION AT GENERAL MEETING

THAT the directors recommend to the annual general meeting of the company to be held on   that   be appointed additional directors of the company in the places of   who resigned on   19   .

7.1.7 APPOINTMENT OF CHAIRMAN

THAT   be appointed chairman of the board.

7.1.8 APPOINTMENT OF SECRETARY

THAT   be appointed secretary of the company [at a salary payable from   19   at the rate of £   per annum], such appointment being terminable by three months' notice in writing given by either party to the other at any time.

7.1.9 APPOINTMENT OF CORPORATE REPRESENTATIVE

THAT   or, failing him,   or, failing him,   be appointed, pursuant to section 375, Companies Act 1985, to act as the company's representative at any meeting of the members or creditors of other companies in which the company is or may hereafter become interested as a member or creditor.

7.1.10 CHANGE IN REGISTERED OFFICE

THAT the registered office of the company be changed from   to   and the secretary be instructed to file form 287 at the Registry forthwith.

7.1.11 ADOPTION OF SEAL

THAT the seal, of which an impression is affixed in the margin hereof, be adopted as the common seal of the company.

7.1.12 TO APPROVE DOCUMENTS SEALED

THAT the affixing of the common seal of the company to the documents set out against items nos   to   inclusive in the seal book be confirmed.

7.1.13 CHANGE OF ACCOUNTING REFERENCE DATE

THAT the accounting reference date of the current and all subsequent accounting reference periods be changed to   and that the current accounting reference period is to be treated as [shortened] and to have come to an end on   .

7.1.14 NUMBERING OF SHARES

THAT all the shares of the company in issue shall henceforth cease to bear distinguishing numbers.

FOR NOTES TO 7.1 SEE PAGE 160

7.1.15 TO APPROVE SHARE TRANSFER

THAT a transfer of   shares of £   each from
to   be approved and that the transferee be entered in the
register of members as the holder of such shares, and that a share certificate be sealed
and issued to the transferee.

7.1.16 TO REFUSE TO REGISTER A TRANSFER

THAT the transfer by   to   of
shares of £   each be refused and that   be notified
forthwith.

7.1.17 TO APPROVE ANNUAL ACCOUNTS

THAT the balance sheet dated   , the profit and loss
account to that date and the directors' report be approved. That the balance sheet be
signed on behalf of the board by two directors and that the directors' report be signed
on behalf of the board by the secretary.

7.1.18 TO CONVENE AN ANNUAL GENERAL MEETING

THAT the annual general meeting for   19   be
held on   19   at
          a.m./p.m. at   .

7.1.19 DIVIDEND RESOLUTIONS

THAT it be recommended to the annual general meeting of the company that a
dividend of   per ordinary share be declared.

THAT an interim dividend for the year ended   19
of   pence per share on the ordinary shares of £1 each of the company be paid
on   19   to shareholders registered at the close of
business on   19   .

7.1.20 CAPITALISATION OF DIRECTORS' LOAN ACCOUNT

THAT the sum of £   being the whole of the company's indebtedness
to   be utilised in making payment in full for   shares of £1
each in the company which are hereby allotted to   and that he
be entered in the register of members as the holder of such shares and a share
certificate be sealed and delivered to him.

7.1.21 APPROVAL OF CONTRACT FOR ALLOTMENT OF SHARES FOR NON-CASH CONSIDERATION

There was produced an engrossment of an agreement between
and the company providing for the transfer to the company of the plant and
machinery shown in the schedule thereto in consideration of the allotment
to   of   shares of £1 each, credited as fully
paid.

THAT the said agreement be approved and that the common seal of the company be
affixed to the engrossment thereof.

FOR NOTES TO 7.1 SEE PAGE 160

7.1.22 RESOLUTION TO MAKE A CALL

THAT a call of   pence per share be made on the   issued ordinary shares of £1 each, such call to be payable on or before   19   at the company's registered office.

7.1.23 TO DEMAND PAYMENT OF UNPAID CALL

THAT a notice be sent to   requesting payment of the sum of £   being payment in respect of the call made on   19   and notifying him that if payment is not made within 14 days from the date of service of the notice the   ordinary shares of £1 each registered in his name will be forfeited.

7.1.24 TO FORFEIT SHARES

THAT   ordinary shares of £1 each in the company   pence paid up and registered in the name of   of   be forfeited for non-payment of the final call of   pence per share payable on or before   19   , due notice of which was given to the said shareholder on   19   in accordance with minute number   of the board meeting held on   19   and also on   19   in accordance with minute number   of the board meeting held on   19   ;
AND THAT the shares be sold, disposed of or reissued in such manner as the directors shall determine.

7.1.25 TO SELL FORFEITED SHARES

THAT the ordinary shares of £1 each registered in the name of which shares have been forfeited be sold to   of   for £   and that a certificate be issued to   credited fully paid.

7.1.26 TO CONVENE AN EXTRAORDINARY GENERAL MEETING

THAT an extraordinary general meeting of the company be convened at which the following resolutions shall be proposed:

AND THAT the members be requested to agree to holding the meeting being held on short notice.

The secretary was instructed to give the notice of the meeting to the members of the company entitled thereto and to the company's auditors.

NOTES ON 7.2

The Act does not contain provisions authorising a director to appoint an alternate director to act on his behalf in his absence, and accordingly alternates may only be appointed if the articles of association contain a specific provision – see regulations 65 to 69 of Table A. The wording of Table A provides for the alternate either to be an existing director of the company or to be a person approved by the board. **7.2** contains precedents for the appointment and revocation of appointment of an alternate director.

For the purposes of s.741, an alternate director is regarded as being a director of the company. He is legally responsible for his own acts as a director and he is subject to all the statutory obligations imposed on directors. The particulars of alternate directors should be entered in the register of directors and should be filed with the Registrar on form 288.

ALTERNATE DIRECTORS

7.2.1 FORM OF APPOINTMENT OF ALTERNATE DIRECTOR

Pursuant to article   of the articles of association of
Limited and subject to the approval of a majority of the directors, I,
              , being a director of   Limited, hereby
appoint   , of   , to be my alternate director.

(Signature)

(Address)

(Date)

7.2.2 FORM OF REVOCATION OF APPOINTMENT OF ALTERNATE DIRECTOR

Pursuant to article   of the articles of association of
Limited, I,   , hereby revoke the appointment dated
              19   of   as my alternate director
of   Limited.

(Signature)

(Address)

(Date)

7.2.3 RESOLUTION APPROVING APPOINTMENT OF ALTERNATE DIRECTOR

There was produced a form of appointment dated
19   by which   appoints   to be his
alternate director.

Resolved:
    THAT the appointment by   of   to
        be his alternate director be approved.

7.2.4 BOARD MINUTE NOTING REVOCATION OF APPOINTMENT OF ALTERNATE DIRECTOR

A form of revocation dated   19   by which
              revokes the appointment of   as his alternate
director was produced and noted.

NOTES ON 7.3

Under ss. 303 and 304, a company may by ordinary resolution remove a director at any time regardless of anything to the contrary in the articles of association or in any agreement with the director (but without prejudice to any right he may have for compensation or damages).

Special notice (see s.379) must be given to the company of the intention to propose such a resolution, and a copy of such notice must be sent to the director concerned, who may make representations in writing to the company and may requisition their circulation to the members of the company. **7.3** contains specimens of the special notice to be given to the company and the notice to be given by the company to the members.

Should the company receive such special notice, considerable care should be taken that the requirements of ss. 303 and 304 are strictly complied with and it may be considered appropriate to take legal advice.

REMOVAL OF DIRECTOR

7.3.1 SPECIAL NOTICE TO REMOVE A DIRECTOR

The Directors,

Limited

I hereby give notice, pursuant to sections 303 and 379, Companies Act 1985, of my intention to propose the following resolution as an ordinary resolution at the next [annual/extraordinary general] meeting of the company.

RESOLUTION

THAT   be removed from his office of director of the company.

(*Signature*)

(*Address*)

(*Date*)

7.3.2 NOTICE TO BE GIVEN BY THE COMPANY TO REMOVE A DIRECTOR

Included in the notice of the [annual general] meeting will be the following item of business:

To consider the following resolution which will be proposed as an ordinary resolution, special notice having been given pursuant to sections 303 and 379, Companies Act 1985.

RESOLUTION

THAT   be removed from his office of director of the company.

NOTES ON 7.4

This clause can be useful to include in a company's articles where a company wishes to enhance the status of certain key employees without appointing them to the board of directors. A divisional director appointed pursuant to this provision is not deemed to be a director within the meaning of the Act and therefore the requirements of the Act with regard to the register of directors etc., do not apply to such appointments.

APPOINTMENT OF DIVISIONAL DIRECTOR

'The directors shall have power from time to time by resolution to appoint any one or more persons to the office of divisional director of the company and the following provisions with regard to any such appointment or appointments shall have effect:

1.　the appointment, tenure of office, remuneration (if any) and scope of duties of a divisional director shall be determined from time to time by the directors with full power to make such arrangements as they think fit; and the directors shall have the right to enter into any contracts on behalf of the company or transact any business of any description without the knowledge or approval of a divisional director, except that no act shall be done that would impose any personal liability on any divisional director except with his full knowledge and consent;

2.　the directors may also from time to time remove any divisional director from office and if they so decide appoint another in his place, but any such removal shall take effect without prejudice to the rights of either party under any agreement between the divisional director and the company;

3.　the appointment of a person to be a divisional director may be in place of or in addition to his employment by the company in any other capacity but unless otherwise expressly agreed between him and the company the appointment as divisional director shall not affect the terms and conditions of his employment by the company in any other capacity whether as regards duties, remuneration, pension or otherwise. The office as a divisional director shall be vacated if he becomes of unsound mind or bankrupt or makes any arrangement or composition with his creditors generally, or becomes prohibited by law from being concerned or taking part in the management of the company, or if he resigns his office or is removed from office by a resolution of the board;

4.　a divisional director shall not be or be deemed to be a director of the company within the meaning of the word as used in the Companies Act 1985 or these articles and no divisional director shall be entitled to attend or be present at any meetings of the board or of any committee of directors unless the directors shall require him to be in attendance;

5.　a divisional director shall attend meetings of the directors and of any committee of the directors whenever called upon to do so and shall at all times be ready to give the directors the benefit of his knowledge, experience and advice.'

NOTES ON 7.5

The precedents contained in **7.5** deal with the appointment, resignation and removal of auditors.

The first auditor of the company may be appointed by the directors, to hold office until the end of the first general meeting at which accounts are laid before the company. If the directors fail to appoint a first auditor, the company in general meeting, may make the appointment (s.384(3)) and **7.5.1**).

At each general meeting at which accounts are laid before the company, the company is required to appoint an auditor to hold office from the conclusion of the meeting until the conclusion of the next such meeting (s.384(1) and **7.5.2**).

Special formalities apply if an auditor other than a retiring auditor is being appointed (ss. 387(2) and 388 and **7.5.5**).

An auditor may resign office by notice in writing (s.390). To be effective, the notice either must state that there are no circumstances connected with the resignation which the auditor considers should be brought to the notice of the members or creditors of the company or must state such circumstances (see **7.5.3**).

Within 14 days of receiving the notice of resignation, the company must send a copy to the Registrar. If the notice contains a statement of circumstances which should be brought to the notice of members or creditors, a copy of the notice must also be sent, within the same time limit, to every person entitled in the normal course to be sent copies of the report and accounts.

The directors are empowered to fill any casual vacancy in the office of auditor (s.384(4)) with effect until the next annual general meeting.

If a company wishes to change its auditor during his term of office, the company may remove the auditor by ordinary resolution (see s.386 and **7.5.4**). Special formalities apply (see ss. 387(2) and 388). Within 14 days of passing the resolution, notice of removal on form 386 must be given to the Registrar.

APPOINTMENT, RESIGNATION AND REMOVAL OF AUDITORS

7.5.1 RESOLUTION FOR APPOINTMENT OF FIRST AUDITORS

THAT   be appointed auditors of the company to hold office until the conclusion of the first general meeting at which accounts are laid before the company.

7.5.2 RESOLUTION (COMPANY IN GENERAL MEETING) FOR PERIODIC REAPPOINTMENT OF AUDITORS

THAT   be reappointed auditors of the company to hold office until the conclusion of the next general meeting at which accounts are laid before the company and that their remuneration be fixed by the directors.

7.5.3 AUDITORS' NOTICE OF RESIGNATION (TO BE DEPOSITED AT THE REGISTERED OFFICE)

To: The directors,

Limited   *Date*

We hereby resign our office as auditors of the company and we confirm that there are no circumstances connected with our resignation which we consider should be brought to the notice of the members or creditors of the company.*

Signed

*If there are such circumstances, for the words from 'we confirm' to the end there should be substituted: 'there are the following circumstances connected with our resignation which we consider should be brought to the notice of the members or creditors of the company:
'.

7.5.4. RESOLUTION (COMPANY IN GENERAL MEETING) FOR REMOVAL OF AUDITORS

THAT   be removed from office as auditors of the company with immediate effect [and that   be appointed auditors of the company in their place to hold office until the conclusion of the next general meeting at which accounts are laid before the company and that their remuneration be fixed by the directors].

7.5.5 RESOLUTION (COMPANY IN GENERAL MEETING) FOR APPOINTMENT OF AUDITORS OTHER THAN RETIRING AUDITORS

THAT   be appointed auditors of the company in place of the retiring auditors to hold office until the conclusion of the next general meeting at which accounts are laid before the company and that their remuneration by fixed by the directors.

NOTES ON 7.6

If a company is dormant within the meaning of s.252, it may by special resolution (see **7.6.1**) dispense with the appointment of auditors while it remains dormant.

A company is dormant providing it does not enter into a significant accounting transaction. A significant accounting transaction is a transaction in respect of which there is a legal obligation to make an entry in its accounting records.

If a company passes a special resolution dispensing with the appointment of auditors and it remains dormant, it need not appoint auditors nor annex an auditors' report to the annual accounts.

The statement in **7.6.2** must appear immediately above the signatures of the directors required by ss. 238 and 253.

A company ceases to be dormant immediately it enters into a significant accounting transaction and auditors must then be appointed.

DORMANT COMPANIES: EXCLUSION OF APPOINTMENT OF AUDITORS

7.6.1 SPECIAL RESOLUTION TO BE PASSED IN GENERAL MEETING

THAT, the company having satisfied the provisions of section 252, Companies Act 1985, relating to dormant companies, the company be exempt from the obligation to appoint auditors as otherwise required by section 384 of that Act.

7.6.2 STATEMENT ON BALANCE SHEET

The company was dormant within the meaning of section 252, Companies Act 1985, throughout the financial year ended   19   .

GENERAL NOTES ON APPOINTMENT OF DIRECTOR

Action	Notes

1. Before appointment
(a) check articles of association for:
   (i) number of directors permitted
   (ii) qualification shares requirement
   (iii) methods of appointment (e.g. board resolution, shareholders' resolution, letter of appointment from a shareholder entitled by the articles to appoint representative directors, etc.)
(b) ascertain:
   (i) name and address of appointee
   (ii) proposed date of appointment
   (iii) intended method of appointment	

2. Appointment Dependent upon 1(b)(iii) above, draft: (a) board resolution or (b) notice for ordinary resolution for general meeting or (c) notification to board (usually on agenda for next meeting)	

3. Upon appointment
(a) issue to the director (where appropriate):
   (i) service agreement
   (ii) conditions of employment
   (iii) pension scheme documentation
   (iv) share qualification requirements
   (v) share interests guidance notes
 	
   (vi) share dealing rules (if applicable)
 	
   (vii) list of directors
   (viii) memorandum and articles
   (ix) schedule of board meeting dates
   (x) expense claims procedure
   (xi) company organisation notes
(b) obtain from the director:
   (i) present forename(s) and surname
   (ii) any former forenames or surnames
   (iii) usual residential address
   (iv) nationality
   (v) business occupation
   (vi) other directorships held including past directorships if a public company or the subsidiary of a public company
   (vii) Date of birth
   (viii) interests in shares and debentures (within 5 days of appointment)
   (ix) interests in contracts
   (x) tax form P45
	
	(A)
	(A)
	(A)
	
	ss. 324, 328 and Sch. 13, Parts II and III
	(C) ID provisions (if applicable)
	
	(B)
	
	ss. 288, 289 and Sch. 1
	
	ss. 324, 328 and Sch. 13, Parts II and III
	s.317
	(A) (B)

Action	Notes
(xi) primary appointment for NI contributions (xii) bank details for salary/fees (xii) specimen signature (xiv) signature on form 288	**(B)**

4. Notifications
(a) Registrar of Companies (within 14 days)
(b) company's registrar
(c) bankers
    (i) certified copy of board minute
    (ii) specimen signature
(d) company departments and subsidiary companies
(e) auditors
(f) solicitors
(g) merchant bank
(h) Inland Revenue (PAYE)
	Form 288
	
	(A)
	
	(B)

5. Registers Enter requisite information obtained under 3.2 in: (a) register of directors (b) register of directors' interests	
6. Additional notifications in certain cases The following types of company are governed by special regulations: (a) Lloyd's brokers (b) insurance companies (c) banks and deposit takers (d) companies holding consumer credit licences	
Notes (A) Usually not applicable to a non-executive director. (B) Not applicable to an existing employee. (C) Not applicable to an unlisted company.	

GENERAL NOTES ON TERMINATION OF DIRECTOR'S APPOINTMENT

Action	Notes

1. Before appointment
(a) ascertain:
   (i) reason for termination
   (ii) effective date
   (iii) terms
(b) check articles of association for:
   (i) arrangements regarding fees
   (ii) any other regulations regarding termination
	(A)

2. Termination
(a) dependent on 1(a)(i) above, obtain a copy of relevant document (e.g. letter of resignation, notice from shareholder, court order, etc.)
(b) dependent on 2.1, draft:
   (i) notification to board (usually on agenda for next meeting) or
   (ii) special notice for ordinary resolution at general meeting (28 days)	

3. Upon termination
(a) issue to the director:
   (i) letter of acknowledgment of resignation or notification of removal
   (ii) notification regarding financial arrangements
   (iii) tax form P45
(b) obtain from the director:
   (i) memorandum and articles of association
   (ii) any company documents or property
	(B)

4. Notifications (a) The Stock Exchange (immediately) (if applicable) (b) press (if applicable) (c) Registrar of Companies (within 14 days) (d) company's registrar (e) bankers (f) company departments and subsidiary companies (g) auditors (h) solicitors (i) merchant bank (j) Inland Revenue (PAYE)	**(C)** **(C)** Form 288
5. Registers Record date of ceasing to hold office in: (a) register of directors (b) register of directors' interests	
6. Additional notifications in certain cases The following types of company are governed by special regulations: (a) Lloyd's brokers	

Action	Notes
(b) insurance companies (c) banks and deposit takers (d) companies holding consumer credit licences	

Notes:

(**A**)(1) Examples of reasons for termination are:
- (a) retirement (and not offering himself for re-election)*
- (b) resignation*
- (c) failure to take up any share qualification, or disposal of shares which reduces his holding below the qualification level†
- (d) bankruptcy†
- (e) disqualification by a court order (ss. 1–6, CDDA) from being a director, e.g. because of conviction of an offence in connection with company formation or management†
- (f) removal by the company in general meeting under the terms of ss. 303 and 304 and CP, s.14
- (g) death

(2) The company's articles of association may also provide additional grounds, e.g.:
- (h) making a composition with his creditors (i.e. insolvency without bankruptcy)†
- (i) becoming of unsound mind†
- (j) being absent from meetings of directors without leave for a stated period†
- (k) removal by shareholder entitled to appoint and remove representative directors*

* Effected by letter.

† Board takes note of report by secretary (appointment is vacated automatically from date of occurrence).

(**B**) Usually not applicable to a non-executive director.

(**C**) Not applicable to a company whose shares are not traded on the Stock Exchange

GENERAL NOTES ON APPOINTMENT OF SECRETARY

Action	*Notes*
1. Before appointment ascertain: (a) name and address of appointee (b) proposed date of appointment (c) requirements of s.286 are met	 **(A)**
2. Appointment Draft board resolution	
3. Upon appointment (a) issue to the appointee: (i) service agreement (ii) conditions of employment (iii) company organisation notes (b) obtain from the appointee: (i) present forename and surname (ii) usual residential address (iii) signature on form 288	 If appropriate If an individual **(B)** **(B)** **(B)**
4. Notifications (a) Registrar of Companies (within 14 days) (b) The Stock Exchange (c) company's registrar (d) solicitors (e) bankers (i) certified copy of board minute (ii) specimen signature (f) auditors (g) company departments and subsidiary companies (h) press	 Form 288 **(C)** **(A)**
5. Registers Enter requisite information obtained under 3(b) in register of directors and secretaries	
6. Additional notifications in certain cases The following types of company are governed by special regulations: (a) Lloyd's brokers (b) banks and deposit takers (c) companies holding consumer credit licences	

Notes:
(A) Not applicable to a private company.
(B) The information listed is that required where an individual is appointed secretary. Where a corporation or a Scottish firm is appointed secretary, the corporate or firm name and its registered or principal office should be given instead. Where all the partners in a firm are appointed joint secretaries, the name of the firm and the address of its principal office may be stated instead of the particulars in respect of each individual. Form 288 should be signed by a director or partner as appropriate.
(C) Not applicable to a company whose shares are not traded on the Stock Exchange.

GENERAL NOTES ON ALTERATION OF ACCOUNTING REFERENCE DATE

ARD = Accounting reference date
ARP = Accounting reference period

Action	Conditions to be fulfilled

1. **Extension of ARP**	(a) *during current ARP*
	    (i) can be done at any time before the end of the ARP
	    (ii) cannot apply to a previous ARP (except as indicated in 1(b) below)
	    (iii) must not extend the ARP beyond a total of 18 months
	    (iv) can terminate the ARP at a date earlier than the date of the notice to Registrar of Companies (see 1(a)(vi))
	    (v) cannot be altered if the company's ARP has been extended on a previous occasion and less than 5 years has elapsed since that particular ARP came to an end – *unless* the alteration is now to enable the company's ARD to coincide with that of one of its subsidiary companies or of its holding company
	    (vi) notice to be given to Registrar of Companies before the end of the existing ARP on form 225(1), specifying that the ARP is to be extended

	(b) *after the end of an ARP*
	    (i) can apply only where the alteration is to be made to enable the company's ARD to coincide with that of one of its subsidiary companies or of its holding company (no restrictions as regards timing of any previous extensions)
	    (ii) can be done at any time up to the date by which accounts in relation to the ARP must be laid and delivered
	    (iii) cannot apply to a previous ARP
	    (iv) must not extend the ARP beyond a total of 18 months
	    (v) can terminate the ARP earlier than its existing ARD
	    (vi) notice to be rendered to Registrar of Companies prior to date at 1(b)(ii) on form 225(2), specifying that the ARP is to be extended

2. **Shortening of ARP**	(a) *during a current ARP* (i) can be done at any time before the end of the period (no restrictions as regards timing of any previous alterations in ARD)

Action	Conditions to be fulfilled
	(ii) cannot apply to a previous ARP (except as indicated in 2(b) below) (iii) can terminate the ARP at a date earlier than the date of the notice to Registrar of Companies (see 2(a)(iv)) (iv) notice to be given to Registrar of Companies before the end of the ARP on form 225(1), specifying that the ARP is to be shortened
	(b) *after the end of an ARP* (i) can apply only when the alteration is to be made to enable the company's ARD to coincide with that of one of its subsidiary companies or of its holding company (no restrictions as regards timing of any previous alterations in ARD) (ii) can be done at any time up to the date by which accounts in relation to the ARP must be laid and delivered (iii) cannot apply to a previous ARP (iv) can terminate the ARP earlier than its existing ARD (v) notice to be rendered to Registrar of Companies prior to date at 2(b)(ii) on form 225(2), specifying that the ARP is to be shortened

Reference: ss. 225 and 226.

8 Meetings

CONTENTS

NOTES ON 8.1 AND 8.2

8.1 is an example of an agenda for an annual general meeting. **8.2** is an example of a notice convening an annual general meeting.

Section 366 provides that every company must hold a general meeting in each calendar year as its annual general meeting, and that not more than 15 months may elapse between the date of one annual general meeting and the next.

The directors usually convene the annual general meeting (regulation 37 of Table A). Section 369 provides that 21 clear days' notice in writing must be given of an annual general meeting.

The routine business at annual general meetings comprises receiving the report and accounts laid before the meeting as required by the Act, the declaration of a dividend, the election of directors and the reappointment of, and fixing the remuneration of, the auditors. Table A no longer makes a distinction between ordinary and special business.

8.2 indicates the nature of the business to be transacted. More detailed information should be given in the notice of meeting of non-routine business, including the text of any resolutions to be proposed.

AGENDA FOR ANNUAL GENERAL MEETING

LIMITED

AGENDA for   ANNUAL GENERAL MEETING for
19   , to be held at   on   day,   19

1. The secretary to read the notice convening the meeting.

2. The representative of the auditors to read the report of the auditors.

3. The chairman to address the meeting and to propose:
   THAT the report of the directors and the audited accounts for the year ended 19   , now laid before the meeting, be received and that the final dividend of   pence per share recommended therein be declared payable on   19   to holders of ordinary shares registered at the close of business on   19 .
             to second the resolution.
   The chairman to invite questions and, having replied, to put the resolution to the meeting and declare the result.

4. The chairman to propose:
   THAT   , the director retiring by rotation, be re-elected a director of the company.
             to second the resolution.
   Put to the meeting and declare the result.

5.   , having given special notice pursuant to sections 293(5) and 379 of the Companies Act 1985, to propose:
   THAT   , who has attained the age of 70 years, on 19   , be re-elected a director of the company.
             to second the resolution.
   Put to the meeting and declare the result.

6.   , a member, to propose:
   THAT   be reappointed auditors of the company to hold office until the conclusion of the next general meeting at which accounts are laid before the company and that their remuneration be determined by the directors.
             , another member, to second the resolution.
   Put to the meeting and declare the result.

7. The chairman to propose as a special resolution:
   THAT the articles of association of the company be altered by deleting the word 'two' in the third line of article   and inserting the word 'three' in its place.
             to second the resolution.
   The chairman to invite questions and, having replied, to put the resolution to the meeting and declare the result.

8. The chairman to close the meeting.

FOR NOTES TO 8.2 SEE PAGE 188

NOTICE CONVENING ANNUAL GENERAL MEETING

LIMITED

NOTICE IS HEREBY GIVEN that the annual general meeting of the company for
19   will be held at   on
19   at   a.m./p.m. for the following purposes:

1. To receive the report of the directors and the audited accounts for the year ended   19   (and to declare a dividend).

2. To elect directors in place of those retiring (see directors' report).

3. To appoint the auditors.

4. To authorise the directors to fix the remuneration of the auditors.

5. To transact any other ordinary business of the company.

BY ORDER OF THE BOARD

Secretary

Dated

Registered office

Note: A member entitled to attend and vote at the above meeting is entitled to appoint a proxy to vote instead of him. A proxy need not be a member of the company.

NOTES ON 8.3

An extraordinary general meeting may, subject to the articles, be convened at any time for the transaction of business which requires attention before the next annual general meeting.

The directors are by regulation 37 of Table A empowered to convene extraordinary general meetings whether they themselves instigate the meeting or whether they are required to call the meeting by a requisition lodged under s.368 (see **8.4**).

The only business which may be validly transacted at an extraordinary general meeting is the business specified in the notice convening the meeting. The type of resolution — ordinary, special or extraordinary — should be specified in the notice. Unless consent to short notice is given (see **8.6**) 21 clear days' notice must be given if a special resolution is proposed, and 14 days' notice must be given if an ordinary or extraordinary resolution is proposed (ss. 369 and 378).

In every notice convening a meeting there must appear with reasonable prominence a statement that a member entitled to attend and vote is entitled to appoint a proxy to attend and vote instead of him, and that the proxy need not also be a member (s.372).

NOTICE CONVENING EXTRAORDINARY GENERAL MEETING

LIMITED

NOTICE IS HEREBY GIVEN that an extraordinary general meeting of the above-named company will be held at   on
19   at   a.m./p.m. for the purpose of considering and, if thought fit, passing the following resolution which will be proposed as an ordinary/special/extraordinary resolution:

BY ORDER OF THE BOARD

Secretary

Dated

Registered office

Note: A member entitled to attend and vote at the above meeting is entitled to appoint a proxy to vote instead of him. A proxy need not be a member of the company.

NOTES ON 8.4 and 8.5

A member or members of a company with a share capital holding not less than one-tenth of the paid-up capital carrying voting rights may at any time lodge a requisition requiring the directors to convene an extraordinary general meeting for the purposes stated in the requisition (s.368).

On receipt of the requisition the directors must, within 21 days, convene the meeting. If the directors do not comply with this requirement, the requisition-ists (or any of them representing more than one-half of the voting rights of all of them) may convene the meeting at any time within three months from the date of deposit of the requisition (**8.5**).

If the directors proceed to call the meeting, the notice will be in the form of **8.3**.

REQUISITION OF GENERAL MEETING

To the directors of   LIMITED

We, the undersigned, being members of the above-named company holding in the aggregate   ordinary shares of £   each out of the issued paid-up capital of   ordinary shares of £1 each, require you, pursuant to section 368 of the Companies Act 1985, to convene an extraordinary general meeting of the company for the purpose of considering the following resolutions, which will be proposed as ordinary resolutions:

RESOLUTIONS

Dated

Signed

FOR NOTES TO 8.5 SEE PAGE 194

NOTICE OF REQUISITIONED MEETING GIVEN BY REQUISITIONISTS

LIMITED

NOTICE IS HEREBY GIVEN that, pursuant to a requisition dated
19   made in accordance with the provisions of section 368 of the Companies Act 1985, and deposited at the registered office of the company on   19   , an extraordinary general meeting of the company will be held at   on
19   , at   a.m./p.m. for the purpose of considering the following resolutions, which will be proposed as ordinary resolutions:

RESOLUTIONS

(Signatures of requisitionists)

Dated

Registered office

Note: A member entitled to attend and vote at the above meeting is entitled to appoint a proxy to vote instead of him. A proxy need not be a member of the company.

NOTES ON 8.6

Section 369 is useful where it is not possible to give the requisite period of notice of meeting. This provision enables the calling of a meeting at shorter notice than the minimum period allowed by the Act or by the articles; it does not allow for the giving of notice to be completely dispensed with.

8.6.1 contains a consent to short notice for an extraordinary general meeting at which a special resolution is proposed and **8.6.3** contains a consent to short notice for an extraordinary general meeting at which an ordinary resolution is proposed. The consent must be signed by the proportion of members indicated therein. Several copies of this agreement, in like form, may be prepared if it is not convenient to obtain all the signatures on one form.

If consent to short notice is required for an annual general meeting all the members of the company must consent (see **8.6.2**).